Strategic Participatory Communication and Development

There has been a recent shift in the nature of public engagement from a culture of paternalism and control towards a public-centred approach involving collaboration and co-creation. This book draws on public relations and development communication insights to build a new community engagement model for public sector organisations who wish to engage with rural communities in developing countries. This theoretical model also offers a practical framework for Government in particular to engage with and empower rural communities as they adopt and exploit infrastructure developments. The outcome is mutual benefit.

By examining in detail how Government communicates with rural communities on renewable energy infrastructure projects in Indonesia, and underpinned by empirical research with those communities, this new participatory framework has been developed. It envisages progressive empowerment of rural communities as Government encourages active engagement on the installation and exploitation of renewable energy. This entails encouraging communities to determine for themselves their uses of sustainable energy sources and to take ownership of a co-determined future. In so doing, the Government itself is more likely to achieve its own renewable energy commitments.

Research-based and combining theory with practice, this thought-provoking book will be welcomed by strategic communication and public relations scholars and practitioners alike.

Anne Gregory, Emeritus Professor of Corporate Communication at the University of Huddersfield, is the author of over 100 books, book chapters and academic and popular journal articles. Professor Gregory is an Adjunct Professor at LSPR Communication and Business Institute, Jakarta, Indonesia, and at RMIT University, Melbourne, Australia.

Professor Gregory is a Board member of the Chartered Institute of Public Relations and serves on its International Committee and AIinPR Panel. She is also a former Chair of the Global Alliance and directed the worldwide work on developing the Global Capability Framework for the public relations and communication management profession. She is the Director of Practix Limited, a research and training consultancy.

Dr. Gregory holds the CIPR Sir Stephen Tallents Medal for her outstanding contribution to the profession, the US Institute for Public Relations Distinguished Pathfinder award for research, the Public Relations Society of America's Atlas Award for her international work, the Canadian Public Relations Society's Outstanding Achievement Award, the European Public Relations Research and Education Association's (EUPRERA) Distinguished Scholar Award for her contribution to the European body of knowledge and the International Association for the Measurement and Evaluation of Communication's (AMEC) Dom Bartholomew Award in recognition of outstanding service to the communication measurement and evaluation industry.

Gregoria Arum Yudarwati is Professor of Communications, at Universitas Atma Jaya Yogyakarta, Indonesia. Her research interests are on public relations, community engagement and sustainability communication. Most of her research projects have been recognised and supported by international funders, including the Australian Government (1999, 2005 and 2015), British Council, UK (2014 and 2016), Arthur W. Page Center, USA (2015, 2021 and 2022) and the Pulitzer Center, USA (2022).

Professor Yudarwati is a senior expert on communication at Kiroyan Partners, a research-based public affairs and strategic communications consulting firm in Indonesia. She has also been appointed as a member of the UK Research and Innovation (UKRI) International Development Peer Review College, which has enriched her insights on the international development agenda.

Strategic Participatory Communication and Development

Engagement and Empowerment

Anne Gregory and Gregoria Arum Yudarwati

Routledge
Taylor & Francis Group

LONDON AND NEW YORK

First published 2025
by Routledge
4 Park Square, Milton Park, Abingdon, Oxon OX14 4RN

and by Routledge
605 Third Avenue, New York, NY 10158

Routledge is an imprint of the Taylor & Francis Group, an informa business

© 2025 Anne Gregory and Gregoria Arum Yudarwati

British Library Cataloguing-in-Publication Data
A catalogue record for this book is available from the British Library

ISBN: 978-1-032-71603-9 (hbk)
ISBN: 978-1-032-83038-4 (pbk)
ISBN: 978-1-003-50744-4 (ebk)

DOI: 10.4324/9781003507444

Typeset in Times New Roman
by KnowledgeWorks Global Ltd.

From Anne: to all my colleagues and friends in Indonesia. You have taught me all I know about your incredible country and so much about generosity, graciousness and resilience.

From Gregoria: to my parents, R.S. Subalidinata and A. Siti Kolimah, who keep reminding me to maintain local wisdom while striving for excellence.

Contents

List of figures

List of tables

Preface

The shift in global economic power is there for all to see: it is moving from the North and West to the South and East. Emerging and developing nations are shaking off the vestiges of colonialism and finding their own way in the world. They have young, aspiring populations and a desire to share in the prosperity that they have observed in Western nations. The temptation and many of the drivers are to 'do things' the way the West has pioneered. Many of the global technology companies are still Western-owned and are seen as the pinnacle of Western capitalist endeavour.

There are, however, many differences and challenges facing these nations. Many are experiencing rapid urbanisation, as their Western forebears did two centuries ago. They share the challenges of technological advancement, climate change, nature depletion and political differences. They are trying to preserve their unique values and cultures, yet the tools in the development locker are overwhelmingly Western and rationalistic.

This book seeks to address one part of the development of jigsaw. It seeks to answer a number of key questions: how do rural communities in emerging and developing nations develop in ways that are not there just to serve national Government and international donor agendas? How are their voices and agendas heard in the drive for economic advancement? How can their local knowledge be used for their own and wider benefit? How can they be transformed from passive participants in their own development, to empowered directors of it?

This book proposes a Strategic Participatory Communication Framework to do this. Based on research in rural hamlets in Indonesia, but adaptable to other emerging and developing economics, this marries the legitimate national aspirations for development with the aspirations of rural communities. Its main contention is that communities become empowered and self-determining through participatory communication, which must become a recognised and embedded part of the development process. The book not only explains the research and thinking behind the model but also offers a practical blueprint for its enactment.

Suitable for those involved in development projects, Masters and undergraduate students in development studies and public relations and communication studies, it offers concise theoretical insights and practical advice and is especially suitable for those seeking a career in development work.

Acknowledgements

We would like to acknowledge the many people who have helped us academically and practically in more ways than they will ever know as we have gone through the journey of writing this book.

First, we would like to thank our colleagues and friends who helped us in the administration and preparation for and the undertaking and writing up of the field research in the Island of Java, Indonesia: Dr Maura Cresentiana Ninik Sri Rejeki, Ignatius Agus Putranto, Fransisca Anita Herawati, Lukas Deni Setiawan, Pupung Arifin, Ina Nur Ratriana and up to January 2018, Dr Johanna Fawkes. The British Council Institutional Links Newton Fund provided us with generous financial support through a competitive grant. Our employers, the University of Huddersfield, United Kingdom, who were the grant holders, and Universitas Atma Jaya Yogyakarta, Indonesia, for their support and encouragement throughout. This research would have never have been possible without the time, knowledge and generosity of the people of Kalisonggo, Blumbang and Kedungrong hamlets – terima kasih.

Anne would like to thank her friend and colleague Gregoria for her professionalism, hard work, endless enthusiasm and for constantly striving for the best: she is an inspiration. Gregoria would like to send great appreciation to her mentor and friend Anne for her unwavering support and invaluable knowledge, for helping her navigate through challenging times and for believing in her: Anne is not only a world-renowned scholar but also a role model.

This research was supported by British Council Institutional Links Newton Fund Grant ID 217488952 – Indonesia (*Transitions towards Renewable Energy Based Communities: A Strategic Communication and Community Engagement Approach to the Indonesian Energy Self-Sufficient Villages Project*).

List of abbreviations and translations

Adat	Tradition
ASEAN	Association of Southeast Asian Nations
CSR	Corporate Social Responsibility
Dusun	Hamlet
ESG	Environmental, Social and Governance
FGD	Focus Group Discussion
FS	Feasibility Study
Gotong royong	Collective mutual help
Getok tular	Word of Mouth
IBEKA	People-Centred Economic and Business Institute
IT	Information technology
Karang Taruna	Youth group
KKLPMD	Kelompok Kerja Lembaga Pemberdayaan Masyarakat Dusun/ Working Group of Dusun's Community Empowerment Institute
K-Pop	South Korean popular music
MHPP	Micro-Hydro Power Plant
Musyawarah Rencana Pembangunan (Musrenbang)	Multi-stakeholder discussion of village development planning
Ngayah	Collective mutual help
NGO	Non-Government Organization
PUPESDM	Dinas Pekerjaan Umum, Perumahan, Energi dan Sumber Daya Mineral/ Department of Public Works, Housing, Energy, and Mineral Resources
SDGs	Sustainable Development Goals

Tri Hita Karana	Balinese spiritual philosophy of harmony with God, others and the environment
UK	United Kingdom
UN	United Nations
WOM	Word of Mouth

1 Introduction

This book argues for and introduces an alternative approach to community engagement in the Global South. At its core is a model that has been developed through empirical research in Indonesia and which required deep community engagement. We contend the model has relevance, not only in the Indonesian archipelago and the ASEAN region, but in similar emerging and developing economies whose communities share similar characteristics. It is deliberately designed to be adaptable to their specific needs and contexts, and it is important that those differences are honoured.

Prevailing approaches to community engagement in the ASEAN region

To date, community engagement in the ASEAN region, particularly in the context of rural development, has tended to be based on 'telling and selling'. Telling communities about development plans that others have decided are best for them and persuading them to comply with those plans. The tellers and sellers can be Governments or other donor organisations. Their intentions are usually well-meaning, but the way they go about their projects does not always yield the best community support or achieve the objectives that the planners have set.

This book argues that this is not the best way to proceed. Telling and selling forfeits the opportunity to *collaborate* with communities and thereby gain access to the vast local knowledge they have. It denies valuable *feedback* to development planners, which would improve their plans and reduce potential points of conflict with communities, and it *diminishes* the status of local communities to that of passive recipients rather than active participants in their own future.

The book is grounded in the realities of rural life and a great deal of learning by us as authors. It springs from a two-year project funded by the British Council in Indonesia[1]: the largest country in the ASEAN region. Briefly, the project was about installing micro hydro plants in hamlets (called *dusun* in

DOI: 10.4324/9781003507444-1

Indonesia), so that issues with electricity supply and their economic growth could be solved. We found that villagers had no say in whether or where these plants were installed, and almost none on how they should be used or maintained. The project, which included the research team working with local communities in three hamlets over a two-year period, examined how a deliberative communication strategy could be embedded as part of the two-year installation and community adoption plan in order to maximise the potential for both communities and Government. At the heart of the project were three issues: how these micro hydro installations can:

- be managed so that maximum benefit can be derived from the knowledge of both local communities and Government;
- be introduced and exploited in ways that are beneficial to the aspirations of local communities;
- generate management and strategic information to the Government so that their policies can be adjusted and changed to best meet their own objectives.

These learnings are transferable to other types of projects within that country, and others in the ASEAN region, and potentially to any emerging and developing rural nation.

Central to engagement with rural communities are deep issues of power and empowerment, culture and allocation and distribution of resources. While a whole book could be written on these topics, this is not our focus here, although we will explore them to a limited extent.

From the outset, we acknowledge that there are many different contexts for and concepts of community engagement. Contexts cover concerns about governance and decision-making in very different fields, from science and technology, to health, environment and land use and planning.[2]

Engagement in densely populated urban areas is different from that in more sparsely populated and dispersed rural communities. Engagement practices will vary given the culture in which it takes place – engagement in New York is necessarily very different from in New Guinea.

'Engagement' ranges across a continuum of responses from complete ignorance to complete involvement. There is general agreement that at its best, engagement should empower communities to participate in the decision-making process. This involves working collaboratively with and through groups of people. However, it is impossible to ignore an instrumentalism which considers engagement as a tool to achieve organisational or Government goals and that reality is the more dominant in practice.[3]

This book does not enter the contested debates over engagement concepts; rather, it focuses on the development of a practical framework which we believe to be of utility whatever the approach. For the purposes of this book, community engagement is taken to mean *publicly available and transparent discussion processes that enable informed citizen involvement in decisions that affect their lives.* Thus, fundamentally, community engagement here is about communication-driven processes that allow organisations (of any type, including Government) to empower communities and to enhance their ability to take and maintain control over their own lives. Such engagement can be facilitated through many types of communication, for example, development communication, corporate communication, public relations or in social media interactions. We would also stress that we do not see engagement as a static and linear process. It continuously evolves and is influenced by a variety of factors such as culture, public expectations, technology and events such as pandemics or natural disasters. It also involves dynamic shifts in power and perceptions of power over time from the initiator to those being engaged. Through its unfolding, engagement prompts a meaningful response by all parties as together they tackle pressing, real-world problems.

Given this book is about a different approach to community engagement in the Global South and that it implicitly suggests Western models may not be adequate, we now examine some of the challenges that brings. As globalisation continues apace, there is a tendency to seek for common solutions to problems and to apply them in every context. This is not just laziness, but where Governments and funding agencies, many of which operate globally, are held to account for how they use their resources, they seek standard approaches which have proved successful elsewhere and which are amenable to standard measures of success. Thus, globalisation sets the backcloth to all work in this area and it was a factor we had to bear in mind in this project. This is especially the case for the objectives set by Government for rural community development. These are usually aligned to global measures of advancement such as economic growth indicators and UN sustainability goals to which nation-states ascribe. There also appear to be 'accepted' ways of working with rural communities, which are along the line of 'tell and sell' as outlined above as common practice in emerging and developing nations.

It is this issue of globalisation then that we explore in some detail next.

The challenges of globalisation

We would argue that globalisation has narrowed our understanding of the variety of organisation-community relationships around the world. Large global conglomerates and institutions require 'corporate ways of doing things' and have systems and processes, including IT systems that imply convergence and a level of homogeneity. Politically, there can be seen to be large blocks who ascribe to similar ideologies: democratic capitalism, autocratic state-directed economies and variations in between. Economic, political and cultural integration as part of the globalisation process has increased interconnectedness.

However, we would contend that globalisation is more often seen through economic and political lenses, rather than how it affects individuals and cultures. Indeed, globalisation has been seen as reinforcing cultural homogenisation throughout the world while also diminishing local cultural values. The globalisation of cultural values and norms has tended to promote Western ideals because they are so ubiquitous in cultural artefacts such as film, mass tourism, fast food chains, sport, books, pop music and television. Despite the emergence of other cultures such as K-Pop from South Korea, even this can be argued as being Western-originated. As a result, sight is lost of local cultural identity and either its importance diminished, or there is a desire to put it to one side.[4] Furthermore, the geographical boundaryless nature of technology has promoted the penetration of Western culture, blurred the boundaries of domestic and regional cultural identities and promoted a global culture that focuses on wealth creation, modernism and consumerism.[5] At the same time, the lack of internet access and digital literacy in some parts of the world has created more social and economic inequality between countries. Data from the International Telecommunication Union, the United Nations specialised agency for information and communication technologies, shows that in 2022, an estimated 2.7 billion people, which is one-third of the world's population, remain unconnected to the internet and reside in less developed countries.[6]

With increased knowledge brought through expanded travel opportunities for individuals and popular culture bringing other cultures right into the home, it would be reasonable to suppose that globalisation would encourage more diverse perspectives. This is not obviously the case.

It is important to mention here, although it will be explored more deeply in Chapter 2, that theories of development and communication have also remained stubbornly rooted in Western rationalism. The dominance of Western book publishing houses and academic journals has led to a Western, i.e. US-Eurocentric paradigm of communication theories.[7] It is argued that these 'Western' oriented theories are insufficient to understand or explain local phenomena in different parts of the world. In journalism studies, for instance, more studies are conducted and derived from Global North countries, which represent around 14% of the global population. Findings from research such as this are, however, usually assumed to reflect global trends and are rarely contextualised into different contexts.[8] Likewise, scholars in public relations and strategic communication have argued for more global input and perspectives.[9] This would include research into multinational companies who allocate resources to engage with communities in order to understand local culture and thereby gain community acceptance and legitimacy.

Within this globalised world, local communities are not well-served because the models of community engagement, primarily designed by Western academics and Western organisations, are mostly drawn from Western settings, which are culturally different. Therefore, we have responded to an apparent need to engage in detailed empirical studies to address the limitations of Western perspectives and generate alternatives that take local context into consideration.

Ways to face the challenges

To address this complex and multi-faceted task, this book offers an alternative approach to community engagement – the focus of our attention. It does this in four ways.

First, because we undertook extensive field studies in village communities in Indonesia over two years, it broadens the empirical research base upon which to draw localised conclusions and recommendations. It allowed time for critical analysis of current practices and opened up opportunities for new theoretical (as well as practical) approaches. Local phenomena in non-Western countries may surface issues and raise research questions that might be lacking from Western-based studies, but are vital in non-Western countries. For example, unlike most Western countries, Indonesia's political context tends to be more authoritarian,[10] though it can be argued that Indonesia has been in the democratisation process since its reconstitution in 1998. Indonesia is classified as an upper middle-income economy[11] with 42% of its 260 million population living in rural areas. Culturally, Indonesia is the home of an estimated 50 to 70 million indigenous people with 1,331 ethnic groups recognised by the Government.[12] These factors lead to a unique mix of challenges and needs which shape the way the Government as well as organisations engage with their communities. We learned about and from these factors and were able to draw some specific and general lessons that provide more evidence to understand the complexities of conducting community engagement., particularly in the Global South.

Second, this book addresses directly the thorny issue of the different objects and subjects of the study. The essential assumption is that analytical subjects as well as objects of study reflect circumstances within societies where knowledge is produced. As most previous studies are from the West, the object and subject of engagement are mostly from modern organisations, in modern and urban areas. They also tend to be being more organisational-centric than public-centric. The organisation and the public, urban and rural and modern and traditional offer very different challenges and problems. Using a case study of Government communication and engagement in Indonesia, this book, offers a more public-centric approach by exploring the voices of rural communities as the *subject* of the study. These communities and their voices are integral to the study and without them the study cannot exist. This is important because in many considerations of community development and empowerment, communities are the *object* of study. They are separate from it, something 'other' to be observed and decisions made about them, which may or may not see them as having influence in decision-making.

Third, this book explores perspectives which might be absent in Western settings. Social stratification, for instance, is acceptable in collectivist communities, while it is not in the West where diversity, equity and inclusion are currently high on the social agenda. In collectivist communities, local leaders have strong power to influence community decision-making: power distance is accepted as part of community culture. Religion, its values and leaders are significant in directing community fundamentals, such as how to conduct life and what constitutes identity. Within this cultural context, if communication aims for social change, then culture as well as religion become central to the process. For instance, during the COVID-19 pandemic, vaccine uptake in countries with majority Muslim populations was shaped by their religious values, i.e. whether the vaccine was halal or not was a crucial factor.[13] Governments' health communication strategies cannot just ignore religious values; indeed, communication should not just be sensitive to culture, but culture, including religious values are at the *centre* of communication itself.[14] This is unlike in Western settings where the influence of religion and culture more broadly in designing and managing community engagement and communication strategies, are rarely so important.

Finally, this book involves reflexivity. We, the authors, come from two different cultural backgrounds: Europe and Asia. We conducted our study on community-based renewable energy in Indonesia while also learning from similar initiatives in the UK. We observed directly the dynamics, differences and similarities in terms of challenges and culture. We had opportunities to examine feelings, thoughts and intellectual training, and how these shape our analytical thinking as well as reflecting on expert-informed advice on how certain situations should be approached. The engagement process was a learning experience significantly different from that experienced by both authors who have studied and researched in Western countries. When we conducted our study in Indonesian villages, we had to ask permission from local leaders. Once approval was gained, communities then became open and did not hesitate to allocate time to meet. This is common in a collectivist community, in which leaders decide community goals and direction and others take their cue from them. Individualism and individual decision-making on matters that might affect the wider community is not culturally acceptable.

Understanding this situation, we were cautious about using Western-based rationalistic techniques in conducting our fieldwork. For example, we decided we should avoid one-on-one interviews with community members, as these could be viewed as confrontational and personally challenging. Instead, we chose focus group discussions (FDGs), which were undertaken within existing forums in each hamlet. This was more acceptable because it aligned better with collective culture.

A storytelling approach to data gathering was also in line with the oral culture of the community. As a result, hamlet members spoke with us freely, openly and at some length, which allowed us to gain better quality and quantity of data from them. Unlike in Indonesia, when we visited groups who manage community-based renewable energy initiatives in the UK, we conducted in-depth, individual interviews as they were more confident and articulative in sharing individual opinions and may have felt constrained in their levels of honesty if in an FGD.

To some extent, both communities in Indonesia and UK experience similar challenges in managing technology and in ensuring its sustainability, but the way they manage the challenges are different. Through reflexivity, we understood existing approaches better and calibrated with reflection on the principles of personal and collective engagement, we adjusted our own views on how they could be best used or built on to develop more useful interactions with the different communities. This in turn fed through to the design of our model for community engagement in rural communities.

What we offer in this book is a practical yet theoretically sound model which has been grounded in detailed interactions with the reality of community life and critical peer review. The heart of the book is one very substantive case in which issues and principles were explored and tested. This then led to the construction of a model for future approaches to community engagement, empowerment and ownership, which benefits all parties involved.

Structure of the book

The book is structured to tell the story of the case and the subsequent development of the model. It is organised as follows:

Chapter two looks at the academic research in the field of development communication and describes the two main approaches. *Modernisation* is very much driven by economic development objectives and typifies top-down project planning. Government and/or donors set the objectives for projects and communication is aimed at 'persuading the recipients' to comply with the project schema. In contrast, the *participatory* paradigm sees development communication as generating social change where those 'being developed' have agency and are co-producers of that change. Dialogue and co-creation are critical. We lay out our own approach which recognises utility in combining both models, but emphasises the importance of the indigenous knowledge of communities which is deeply rooted in their environment and their own cultural norms and values.

Chapter three provides background to the research project on which this book is based. It outlines Indonesian Government policy on renewable energy including the role of micro hydro power plants (MHPP) and its approach to development, including moves towards a more participatory style. The chapter also covers the governance of Indonesian civil society with a focus on rural communities and how these considerations have shaped the methodological approach to the empirical research that was conducted in three rural hamlets.

The fourth chapter describes how the research in the three hamlets central to this book was conducted and our review of Government policies and project implementation practices, including those responsible for planning and implementing MHPP projects. We found that the project lifecycle consists of five stages: pre-initiation, initiation, adoption, transition and sustainability. We introduce the three hamlets involved in the empirical research and the project lifecycle stage of MHPP development they had reached. We justify the choice of the case methodology and explain why Appreciate Inquiry is appropriate for use in rural communities. Finally, we describe and justify the data collection methods.

Chapter five reports on the results of the research in the three hamlets and shows that although they were at different stages in the MHPP lifecycle, they all had opinions and/or insights into all five. It is apparent from these findings that each community has a willingness and sees opportunities to be more involved in their MHPP development and to broaden the range of people involved, for the benefit of their own communities and Government. There are practical suggestions on how this might happen.

This leads to chapter six, which introduces the strategic participatory communication framework, based on the evidence collected in the study, that participatory communication should be integrated within the physical installation process. Participatory communication at all stages of the MHPP project life cycle, focusing on dialogue and empowerment, treats communities as active collaborators rather than passive recipients. We would argue that such an approach not only leads to more effective and efficient community development projects, which assists Government meet its economic and energy ambitions, but to the empowerment of community members, who, by embracing MHPP ownership as a means of economic development, enhance their social and cultural identity and, importantly, secure their means to self-determination.

Chapter 7 outlines how six for-profit organisations from different industries face challenges when trying to apply global corporate policy for corporate social responsibility (CSR) programmes in very different nations. We present a second model which has many similar characteristics to the one developed from the MHPP research and which shows how strategic participatory communication principles are relevant and can be adapted and used in different settings and cultures.

To complete the book, chapter eight draws a number of conclusions from the thinking and practice recommendations that have been explored. It also lists a number of key learnings and insights that have been drawn from the research project. These are at both the professional practice and personal level.

Notes

1 As recognised in the Acknowledgements, the research underpinning this project was funded by a British Council Newton Fund Institutional Links Grant.

2 For a more detailed discussion on these topics see Dhanesh, G. S. (2017). Putting engagement in its PRoper place: State of the field, definition and model of engagement in public relations. *Public Relations Review*, 43(5), 925–933; Jelen-Sanchez, A. (2017). Engagement in public relations discipline: Themes, theoretical perspectives and methodological approaches. *Public Relations Review*, 43(5), 934–944; Johnston, K. A. & Taylor, M. (2018). Engagement as communication, pathways possibilities, and future direction. In: K. A. Johnston, & M. Taylor (eds.). *The handbook of communication engagement.* (pp. 1–16). John Wiley & Sons, Inc.: Hoboken, NJ.

3 See Lane, T. & Hicks, J. (2014). Best practice community engagement in wind development. Available: http://cpagency.org.au/wp-content/uploads/2014/03/Attachment-E-Best-practice-community-engagement-in-wind-development-FINAL-V1.0.pdf.; Johnston, K. A., Lane, A. B., Hurst, B. & Beatson, A. (2018). Episodic and relational community engagement implications for social impact and social license. In: K. A. Johnston, & M. Taylor (eds.) *The handbook of communication engagement.* (pp. 169–188) John Wiley & Sons, Inc.: Hoboken, NJ.; Yudarwati, G. A. (2019). Appreciative inquiry for community engagement in Indonesia rural communities. *Public Relations Review*, 45(4), Article 101833.

4 See Kaul, V. (2012). Globalisation and crisis of cultural identity. *Journal of Research in International Business and Management*, 2(13), 341–349; Ullah, A. A. & Ho, H. (2020). Globalisation and cultures in southeast Asia: Demise, fragmentation, transformation. *Global Society*, 35 (2), 191–206.

5 Mirrlees, T. (2020). Global culture. In: M. Filimowicz & V. Tzankova. (eds.) *Reimagining communication: Meaning.* (pp. 117–133) Routledge: New York,NY.

6 The International Telecommunication Union (ITU). 2022. Internet surge slows, leaving 2.7 billion people offline in 2022 [Online]. Available: https://www.itu.int/en/mediacentre/Pages/PR-2022-09-16-Internet-surge-slows.aspx [Accessed].

7 For more on this see, for example, Demeter, M., Goyanes, M., Navarro, F., Mihalik, J. & Mellado, C. (2022). Rethinking de-westernization in communication studies: The Ibero-American movement in international publishing. *International Journal of Communication*, 16, 3027–3046; Miike, Y. & Yin, J. (eds.). (2022). Introduction: Global interventions in search of communication theory in human diversity. *The handbook of global interventions in communication theory*. Routledge; New York, NY.; Wang, G. (2011). Beyond de-westernizing communication research: An introduction. In: G. Wang (ed.) *De-westernizing communication research altering questions and changing frameworks.* (pp. 1–18). Routledge, and Waisbord, S. & Mellado, C. (2014). De-westernizing communication studies: A reassessment. *Communication Theory*, 24(4), 361–372.

8 Mitchelstein, E. & Boczkowski, P. J. (2021). What a special issue on latin America teaches us about some key limitations in the field of digital journalism. *Digital Journalism*, 9(2), 130–135.

9 See Sriramesh, K. & Vercic, D. (2009). *The global public relations handbook: Theory, research, and practice.* Routledge; New York and Valentini, C. (2021). Mapping public relations theory: Concluding reflections and future directions. In: C. Valentini, (ed.) *Public relations* (pp. 615–628). De Gruyter Mouton: New York, NY.

10 Freedom House (2023). Freedom in the World [Online]. Available: https://freedomhouse.org/report/freedom-world [Accessed 1 December 2023].

11 World Bank (2023). World Bank Country and Lending Groups. Available: https://datahelpdesk.worldbank.org/knowledgebase/articles/906519

12 International Work Group for Indigenous Affairs (2023). Indigenous peoples in Indonesia. Available: https://www.iwgia.org/en/indonesia.html [Accessed 1 December 2023].

13 Wong, L. P., Alias, H., Megat Hashim, M. M. A. A., Lee, H. Y., AbuBakar, S., Chung, I., Hu, Z. & Lin, Y. (2022). Acceptability for COVID-19 vaccination: Perspectives from Muslims. *Human Vaccines & Immunotherapeutics*, 18(5), Article 2045855.

14 See Dutta, M. J. & Basu, A. (2011). Culture, communication, and health: A guiding framework. In: T. L. Tompson, R. Parrott & J. F. Nussbaum, (eds.) *The Routledge handbook of health communication* (pp.320–334). Routledge: New York, NY. and Yudarwati, G. A., Putranto, I. A., Ratriyana, I. N. & Parera, P. (2023). Towards an interactive and participatory risk communication: Lessons learned from COVID-19 in Indonesia. *Cogent Social Sciences*, 9(1), Article 2221594.

2 Development communication

To ensure our approach to community engagement in Indonesia was informed and rigorously underpinned, we examined the existing academic literature. This helped us understand the different methodologies used in emerging and developing economies more widely to the type of work we were involved in. It also potentially offered us an option to use an existing approach, which we could use either with or without adaptation.

Because we are looking at community engagement in non-Western nations, especially those in emerging economies, the literature on development communication is helpful. As can be expected, given the field is large, there are many different approaches and theories based on range of epistemologies and ontologies, so we have been selective in our overview here.

For the literature, *development* is usually understood to mean the process by which societal conditions are improved. However, there is much disagreement on what represents 'improvement'. The two most prevalent views on development are the *modernisation paradigm*, which in crude and simple terms, assumes individuals to be passive recipients who are 'developed'. Modernisation emphasises economic and technological improvements as the main indicators of progress. The *participatory paradigm*, views development as a process of social change that involves social and cultural aspects in addition to economic and technological advancement. As is apparent, the paradigm adopted shapes the practice of development communication.

While development and the associated development communication are clearly linked, it is essential to separate the two. Development is an aim, whereas development communication is one of the means by which the aim is achieved. The characteristics of development communication are determined both by the paradigm and the aim. In broad terms, the modernisation paradigm uses development communication to inform and gain compliance to aims determined by those promoting the development. The participatory paradigm uses more collaborative methods such as joint objective setting, participation, mutual sharing and feedback for mutual learning.

DOI: 10.4324/9781003507444-2

The modernisation paradigm and behavioural change model of communication

According to the modernisation paradigm, the sources of under-development lie in traditional culture and information deficits, i.e. the objects of development need to know what and how to develop and to the guided to make the desired change. Exposure to new ideas and practices, it is believed, could help remove traditional attitudes (which are assumed to be not conducive to development) and would result in behavioural transformations embracing of change.[1] Modernisation is seen to be evolutionary, which suggests that development is regarded as directional and cumulative, predetermined and irreversible, progressive and immanent with reference to the nation-state.[2] Accordingly, the goal of communication is to change the behaviour of citizens by infusing modern values, disseminating information and transferring technological innovation. This, in turn, will modernise developing countries and their people. Mass media are the preferred channels for communication: they are trusted to prepare individuals in developing countries for a rapid social change by establishing an appetite for modernisation.[3] The diffusion of innovation, social marketing, health promotion and health education are just a few of the theories which inform this paradigm and their focus is on behavioural change.[4]

To accelerate modernisation, the most common mode of operating is 'the project approach', which is characterised by specific activities designed to address and solve a specific problem or set of problems that are seen to hinder development.[5] Development is managed and operated in a business-like manner and follows the project life cycle. This approach is still dominant since it is considered as a more reliable and measurable way of fulfilling the plans and interests of major decision-makers, often large donors or Governments. These decision-makers define the problem or problems and the solution and instigate a project to resolve it (them). This approach is seen to be efficient in serving the interests of and plans from the decision-makers point of view. However, this 'top down' method is problematic. First, it may lead to lack of support and ownership from the communities who are not only the beneficiaries but are also the main actors in development. It is their communities, indeed, they themselves who will be 'modernized'. Second, it assumes that a certain development problem is linked with a certain solution (too simplistic in defining the problem and the solution and causal link between them) and lacking in bottom-up contributions (not well-informed), which leads to inadequate design, insufficient understanding of local realities, failing to involve relevant stakeholders and to account for their perceptions from the beginning of the project.[6]

While some theorists accept that development can be judged primarily by an increase in production and distribution of capital, the modernisation paradigm has also been criticised as another way to westernise developing economies by embedding Western approaches and institutions and neglecting any alternative routes which may be more appropriate in a given context.[7] Globalisation, discussed in the previous chapter, is very much an expression of this paradigm.

It is not difficult to see the manipulative potential of communication applications within this paradigm. Development targets (communities) are treated as objects of modernisation, rather than actors of social change. Hence, development communication in this paradigm is sender-oriented and media-centric. Mass messages are disseminated with the recipients of those messages being 'out there' and 'targets'. There is a lack of feedback from or listening to communities who find themselves unable to voice their concerns or offer their knowledge. The focus is on persuasion rather than reciprocity and mutual understanding and a potent result is that this can lead to a loss of trust. Decisions become the province of experts and faceless apparatchiks who are detached from the community. Communication is about changing the behaviour or attitudes of the other (those being developed) rather than a joint journey, and the paradigm fails to provide an adequate framework for understanding and achieving social change.

Participatory paradigm and social change model of communication

In response to the inadequacies of the modernisation paradigm, as judged by its limited success, there is an increasing movement to consider changes in human conditions to achieve development. The shift is away from a single-minded focus on economic development to one that is more broadly based on social development. This concentrates on enhancing human potential by removing barriers, working toward improving people's quality of life and giving them freedom to make decisions that they see to be in the community's interest.[8] This development paradigm involves a people-centred process which provides opportunities for them to participate and empowers them to have control over their lives. Such an approach compels a move from seeing individuals as passive recipients to active agents of development, capable of analysing their own situations and developing their own solutions. This shift is important in that it is the community interest, not those of other parties, that is served through development. The driver of this model is the importance of working *with* communities to define their needs and to design and implement programmes to fulfil these needs. This is radically different from an outside actor delineating the problems (often in terms of the priorities of their own agendas) and then imposing a solution intervention on a community.

Communication within this paradigm, accordingly, is not merely about the *transmission* of persuasive information designed to change behaviour. Instead, it is about activating critical reflexivity, dialogue, and consciousness-raising in order that the community is able to articulate problems and solutions that will stimulate social mobilisation and change. Good participative communication is a dialogic process through which communities assert their identity, articulate their aspirations and determine how they can achieve them. Community knowledge and energy applied to a specific issue will have novel outcomes as it is converted into new initiatives. This, in turn, generates new knowledge, which, through collective agreement, will drive change and empower those involved. Co-ownership in setting goals and development plans will secure a sustainable way forwards leading to meaningful outcomes and long-term impact.[9]

Development communication in this paradigm is oriented towards ensuring that the stakeholders in development build trust with and in each other, create mutual understanding, and a vision for the future. Thus, dialogue; collective, inclusive meetings and forums; information sharing; joint working parties and joint decision-processes characterise such communication. This participatory approach has been adopted to support development, however, its definition and practises vary. Not all development is truly participatory, and it can be tokenistic and/or biased toward maintaining the status quo in society.

Both paradigms, social change and project-based development, acknowledge that the involvement of people in the process can lead to change, but their respective operationalisation is different. In sum, in the project-based, sometimes called the institutional approach, participation is largely limited to the implementation stage and used as a tool to achieve pre-determined goals defined by the development agency. For social-change-oriented development initiatives, participation can begin when goals are set and agreed by all those involved and is therefore seen very much as an empowering activity.

Defining accurately what is implied by 'participation' is a major challenge. There are different understandings of what is meant by the term participation and its purpose within the context of development. It is not an absolute concept and can be considered and applied to different degrees and along a continuum. Jules Pretty and colleagues,[10] propose seven different types of participation, ranging from *passive participation*, where people are simply told what is happening and their participation is considered as mere head-counting, to *self-mobilisation*, where people not only have the power to make decisions, but also initiate their own actions. Another four-part classification, proposed by the World Bank[11] is based on the level of stakeholder involvement, i.e. information sharing, consultation, collaboration and empowerment. These types are consistent with Paulo Mefalopulos's classification,[12] which ranges from passive participation, when stakeholders attend meetings to be informed; to empowered participation, when relevant stakeholders take part throughout the whole cycle of the development initiative and have an equal influence on decision-making.

Whatever description of participation is used, it cannot be free from issues of power. Aiming for balanced and equal relationships among donors/Governments and community players is considered unrealistic when hierarchy, castes or inequality are part of the social context. Furthermore, giving up control to enable dialogue is not something those funding development are often willing to do: they have their objectives to meet. There are also concerns about equitable implementation: who should be involved? When? How should it be done?[13] At the very practical level, participation requires flexibility (when, where and at what time), resources to make it happen (facilities, people to organise, travel expenses, etc.) and is time-consuming. These factors cannot be easily estimated or controlled and are often limiters to the participatory process.

The stance of this book

This book does not enter the polarised debate on these two paradigms: modernisation and participatory. Instead, we see utility in both approaches and we bring these perspectives together where we believe the interests of all those involved are best served. The behavioural change communication model through diffusion of innovation and persuasion can be complemented with a social change model of communication, which facilitates the genuine horizontal and vertical participation of all concerned. These positions do not have to be binary. It is perfectly legitimate for Governments and donors to have objectives and many of them do indeed have the good of developing communities as their primary motivator. It is also perfectly legitimate for communities to have their interests and concerns elevated into decision-making and for them to have a say in their own future. An emphasis on one model rather than the other, and not necessarily to the total exclusion of the other, can be useful in different contexts with different goals. Health communication campaigns for increasing vaccine uptake during pandemics, for instance, may be best served using persuasive behavioural change models. Movements which aim for social change, for example, the adoption of new working practices in villages because the electricity supply is now reliable, will be better supported by the participatory model.

This book also acknowledges the vital importance of *indigenous knowledge systems* and takes as a starting point *empowerment* through engagement, dialogue and collective action by all parties. The *process* and the *context* of communication are, in every situation, crucial in development. Development communication in this book is posited on the basis that engagement aims to empower the beneficiaries of development and that this empowerment allows them to self-define what development is in their context and in collaboration with Government and other donors.

The concept of empowerment has been widely used internationally in efforts to address poverty and under-development.[14] Nevertheless, there is no consensus on what empowerment refers to and what it specifically involves although researchers agree it is complex and multi-dimensional.[15] However, there is common agreement, also reflected in this book, that *it is about people, groups or communities gaining control and power over their own lives in their life contexts.*

The case study used in this book is about community engagement in a rural area, using the participatory approach. Participatory communication here is not just about the exchange of information and experiences, but about the exploration and generation of new knowledge aimed at addressing situations that need to be improved.[16] The communication process followed here recognises the importance of cultural identity in local communities as well as participation by all those with a stake in development. Such an approach also helps the Government (in this case) as well as any other organisations involved to comprehend problems that are experienced by communities and with them propose solutions that are significant to all concerned.

We would contend that even though the proposed approach is derived from research in rural areas, the principles identified can be adopted by corporate organisations for other purposes (see Chapter 7). The rapid changes in business ecosystems in the 21st century have driven companies to transform their business into more inclusive and sustainable entities and there is an urgent call for companies to step up on environmental and societal issues.[17] The modernisation and globalisation that they have often desired and driven are under scrutiny for degrading the planet and the well-being of people. Climate change, for instance, has been exacerbated by massive industrialisation and impacts not only the environment, but also the world socio-economically. Those who live in developing countries and mostly in rural areas are those who are most adversely affected by climate change.

Companies also face new accountability pressures, such as that exerted by the sustainability and Environment, Social and Governance (ESG) agendas. Increasing activism demanding that companies embrace more ethical decision-making and action, amplified by an explosion of digital communication technology, is another reason for them to change the way they engage with their stakeholders. Listening, engagement, collaboration and cooperation is the only way for modern organisations to secure their 'licence to operate' and to address the many 'wicked' problems that they and their stakeholders face.

To support this call, this book can contribute in three ways. First, it offers a practical, public-centric and collaborative model of working as opposed to an organisation-centric and top-down one. This latter has dominated development initiatives to date and has not worked as well as wished. The engagement model espoused focuses on communities as the main agents of development. These communities bring their 'whole selves' to the party, including their cultural values and indigenous knowledge. Therefore, inclusive communication is needed to encourage and stimulate conversations and dialogue with them as conscious actors of change.

Second, the book champions people-centred development, which aims for changes in human conditions and fosters holistic well-being rather than economic growth alone. Development is so much more than a growing balance sheet.

Third, this book proposes a practical model and recommendations for community engagement and empowerment with principles that are transferable to the corporate and other sectors. Effective communication in any context allows ordinary people to believe they are empowered to make a difference, and that their contributions are not only desired and valued, but also absolutely necessary.

We contend that the benefits of this approach accrue not just to communities, but to Governments and donors too. In crude terms, they are more likely to achieve their objectives and over the longer term, probably attain more than was originally planned. However, there is no Return on Investment without the Investment being made first, and just as returns are not just financial, neither are the investments. The following chapters will explore these matters in detail.

Notes

1 Melkote, S. R. & Singhal, A. (2021). Communication in development and social change: A genealogy of the field. In: S. R. Melkote, & A. Singhal (eds.) *Handbook of communication and development* (pp.1–14). Edward Elgar Publishing Limited: Cheltenham.

2 Servaes, J. & Malikhao, P. (2008). Development communication approaches in an international perspective. In: J. Servaes, (ed.) *Communication for development and social change* (pp.158–179). Sage: New Delhi.

3 For more on this, see Melkote, S. R. (2018). Communication for development and social change: An introduction. *Journal of Multicultural Discourses*, 13(2), 77–86; Melkote, S. R. & Singhal, A. (2021). Communication in development and social change: A genealogy of the field. In: S. R. Melkote, & A. Singhal (eds.) *Handbook of communication and development* (pp.1–14). Edward Elgar Publishing Limited: Cheltenham and, Waisbord, S. (2018). Family tree of theories, methodologies, and strategies in development communication. In: J. Servaes, (ed.) *Handbook of communication for development and social change* (pp.1–40). Springer Singapore: Singapore.

4 Waisbord, S. (2018). Family tree of theories, methodologies, and strategies in development communication. In: J. Servaes, (ed.) *Handbook of communication for development and social change* (pp.1–40). Springer Singapore: Singapore.

5 Mefalopulos, P. 2008. *Development communication sourcebook, broadening the boundaries of communication.* The World Bank: Washington, DC.

6 Mefalopulos, P. (2003). *Theory and practice of participatory communication: The case of the FAO Project "Communication for Development in Southern Africa".* Doctoral Dissertation, The University of Texas, Austin.

7 Melkote, S. R. & Steeves, H. L. (2015). Place and role of development communication in directed social change: A review of the field. *Journal of Multicultural Discourses,* 10(3), 385–402; Servaes, J. & Malikhao, P. (2008). Development communication approaches in an international perspective. In: J. Servaes (ed.) *Communication for development and social change* (pp.158–179). Sage: (Place of publication needed); Waisbord, S. (2018). Family tree of theories, methodologies, and strategies in development communication. In: J. Servaes, (ed.) *Handbook of communication for development and social change.* (pp.1–40). Springer Singapore: Singapore.

8 For more on the participatory approach see Krys, K., Capaldi, C. A., Uchida, Y., Cantarero, K., Torres, C., Işık, İ., Yeung, V. W. L., Haas, B. W., Teyssier, J., Andrade, L., Denoux, P., Igbokwe, D. O., Kocimska-Zych, A., Villeneuve, L. & Zelenski, J. M. (2022). Preference for modernization is universal, but expected modernization trajectories are culturally diversified: A nine-country study of folk theories of societal development. *Asian Journal of Social Psychology*, 25(4), 731–746. Lie, R. & Servaes, J. (2015). Disciplines in the field of communication for development and social change. *Communication Theory*, 25(2), 244–258; Sen, A. (1999). *Development as freedom*. Oxford University Press: Oxford.

9 Hinthorne, L. L. & Schneider, K. (2012). Playing with purpose: Using serious play to enhance participatory development communication in research. *International Journal of Communication*, 6, 2801–2824. McPhail, T. L. (2009). Introduction to development communication. In: T. L. McPhail (ed.) *Development communication: Reframing the role of the media.* (pp.1–20)Wiley-Blackwell: West Sussex.

10 Pretty, J. N., Gujit, I., Thompson, J. & Scoones, I. (1995). *Participatory learning and action: A trainer's guide.* International Institute for Environment and Development: London.

11 Aycrigg, M. (1998). Participation and the World Bank: Success, constraints, and responses. *Social development paper*. World Bank: Washington.

12 Mefalopulos, P. 2008. *Development communication sourcebook, broadening the boundaries of communication.* The World Bank: Washington, DC.

13 Yudarwati, G. A. (2019). Appreciative inquiry for community engagement in Indonesia rural communities. *Public Relations Review*, 45(4). Article 101833.

14 Martínez, X. Ú., Jiménez-Morales, M., Masó, P. S. & Bernet, J. T. (2017). Exploring the conceptualization and research of empowerment in the field of youth. *International Journal of Adolescence and Youth*, 22(4), 405–418.

15 Hennink, M., Kiiti, N., Pillinger, M. & Jayakaran, R. (2012). Defining empowerment: Perspectives from international development organisations. *Development in Practice*, 22(2), 202–215; Peterson, N. A. (2014). Empowerment theory: Clarifying the nature of higher-order multidimensional constructs. *American Journal of Community Psychology*, 53(1-2), 96–108.

16 Yudarwati, G. A. & Gregory, A. (2022). Improving government communication and empowering rural communities: Combining public relations and development communication approaches. *Public Relations Review*, 48(3). Article 102200.

17 For evidence of these requirements see Konietzko, J., Das, A. & Bocken, N. (2023). Towards regenerative business models: A necessary shift? *Sustainable Production and Consumption*, 38, 372–388; Kopnina, H., Padfield, R. & Mylan, J. 2023. *Sustainable business: Key issues*, Routledge: New York; Lawrence, A., Weber, J., Hill, V. D. & Wasieleski, D. M. (2022). *Business and society: Stakeholders, ethics, public policy.* McGraw Hill: New York, and Raworth, K. 2018. *Doughnut economics: Seven ways to think like a 21st-century economist*, Random House: London.

3 Context of the study

Indonesia has committed to reducing its dependency on fossil fuels and increasing renewable energy as part of its commitment to international climate change agreements – work which began with the 2007 United Nations Climate Change Conference in Bali. Since 2015, the United Nations has included renewable energy as one of its sustainable development goals (SDGs), seeking to provide universal access to clean and sustainable electricity. Indonesia is one of the countries committed to that SDG. At the same time as mainstreaming UN SDGs into its long-term development plan, Indonesia aims to boost its renewable energy sector to improve economic performance at both local and national levels.

Indonesia has introduced a number of policy initiatives to support the global climate change agenda. To achieve its greenhouse gas emission reduction targets by 2050, the Government has designed frameworks and climate change policies that promote renewable energy.[1] As stated in the General National Energy Plan, renewable energy should account for at least 23% of the country's total energy resources by 2025 and 31% by 2050.[2] These commitments and targets have increased Indonesia's expansion of renewable energy technologies, including hydropower technologies. However, there are several challenges, including lack of policy coordination and consistency in governance, high initial costs of equipment and maintenance, inadequate investment in technical research and development, limited support from domestic industry and limited public awareness of renewable energy technologies.

Micro-hydro power plants and the Indonesian renewable energy initiative

Micro-hydro power plants (MHPPs) have been acknowledged for their potential to reduce dependence on fossil fuels. There is no internationally standardised definition of 'micro' hydro power, but in Indonesia this normally refers to a plant capacity of less than 500 kilowatts (kW), which usually provides electricity to households and small businesses.[3] This technology has been recognised for playing a significant role in the economic development of remote

DOI: 10.4324/9781003507444-3

and rural areas in Indonesia and in supporting forest conservation where villagers had previously been dependent on wood for power.[4] Relatively low-cost electricity from MHPPs has also resulted in social changes at both community and household levels. For example, before MHPP were installed in Bawan Valley, Borneo, only around 10% of households had television, so most of them usually watched television with their neighbours. Now, more households own a television and prefer to stay at home, which has led to less social interaction.[5] However, in some communities local schools can remain open after dark and adults are able to study after work which has led to more social interaction.

In rural Indonesia, the topography is hilly and there are plentiful rivers and waterfalls. Streams flow year-round and do not need to be supported from large dams to keep the water supply constant, which makes micro-hydro a sustainable form of energy. Rural communities mostly rely on farming, so they are adept at good water management: they are familiar with water flows for irrigation to support their crops. Even though they do not have formal engineering education, they are 'local experts' who understand local context and potentially can offer practical expertise for local micro-hydro projects.

Development of MHPPs involves state and non-state actors with different interests. State actors include the Ministry of Energy and Mineral Resources, Ministry of National Development Planning, Ministry of Finance, Ministry of Public Works and Public Housing, National Energy Council and local Governments, to name just a few state organisations. Non-state actors include civil organisations, academics and the private sector as well as international donors such as the World Bank and the Asian Development Bank. State actors still hold dominant roles since legally development projects are the responsibility of the Government. However, Government needs to work with non-state actors to undertake tasks they cannot cover, such as to conduct feasibility studies, prepare financing schemes and undertake community engagement.

To manage the complex interplay of all actors, the Government has enacted a multilevel energy governance system, which fits its decentralised Government structure as explained below. This mandates national Government to share authority, knowledge, human resources and funding with local Governments to run its renewable energy programmes. It also allows communities to take part in policy processes.

In line with the decentralised system, community involvement is very important for renewable energy development. For example, the People-Centred Economic and Business Institute (IBEKA) known for its renewable energy project in Subang, West Java, has helped the community to run a 120KW MHPP designed to generate a supply of grid-connected electricity. The local community is involved as a main player and owner, allowing villagers to develop and manage the project. The project is considered successful by many parties and is known for being the first community-based MHPP to connect and sell electricity to the grid, as well as being the first MHPP project.[6]

Indonesian Government development approaches

As discussed in Chapter 2, how Government conduct their development activities is shaped by its underlying philosophy. Development in Indonesia can be categorised into two phases. First, development in the authoritarian era during the New Order (1966–1998) was dominated by the modernisation paradigm. It focused on changing the behaviour of the population in order to gain compliance with pre-determined development goals. During this era Indonesia went through rapid economic development with the Government managing to decrease poverty levels through rural economic development based on agriculture and industrialisation. The terms 'socialization' and 'mobilization' for development programmes were terms used to claim public participation.[7] Mobilisation refers to making people follow courses of action that were pre-determined by the Government. Meanwhile socialisation was more akin to dissemination of information rather than participation. Linear, one-way communication appeared to be the main approach.

Second, since 1998, Indonesia has entered the reformation era as it moves towards a more democratic country. Central to this is the decentralisation policy of 1999, in which power, resources and responsibilities are transferred from central to the regional level of Government. Development projects were included in de-centralisation and since then the Government has launched community-driven development programmes. The shift has been toward 'inclusive' development, which foregrounds equity and justice as well as respect and maintenance of Indonesia's diversity.[8]

Following decentralised principals the Government has laid down development planning procedure, called *Musrenbang* (the Development Planning Meeting). *Musrenbang* acknowledges the importance of participation at all stages of development. This forum combines bottom-up and top-down procedures and tries to marry aspirations from local communities with national long-term planning for development. It also coordinates all stakeholders at local and national levels. *Musrenbang* is conducted at village, district, and regency/city levels to accommodate stakeholders from all strata of Government. In addition to this, all development projects must also conduct a complete risk analysis to explore the possible environmental and social impacts of the proposed project.

Ideally, the *Musrenbang* facilitates organic two-way communication. However, the hierarchical social system in villages and the bureaucratic culture leads to its domination by local elites, politicians, and bureaucrats.[9] The information and knowledge owned by community members attending *Musrenbang* are not based on equality principles. Meetings are mostly attended by males as family leaders and elders. There are discussions and debates, but only between these elites, while other village members who attend are quiet and passive. Accordingly, the *Musrenbang* is tokenistic. Likewise, social and environmental risk assessments become an administrative requirement rather than a thorough impact analysis on communities and environment. These are reasons why several Government projects have failed to gain community support. Instead of involving whole communities and supporting community empowerment, many projects have been regarded as a burden. They are done because Government imposes them on communities and they have no choice.

Indonesian village development and rural governance

There are four levels of Government in Indonesia. The village is the smallest administrative division with district, regency or city, and province in ascending order above them (see Chapter 4, Figure 4.2 for an illustration of how this appears in visual form). According to Indonesia Law No. 6 of 2014, villages have autonomy to regulate and take care of their own businesses and other interests in line with their local customs. Villages also have autonomy to manage and fund local-scale development. In parallel with this, sectoral programmes and regional programmes are conducted together with the district or regency or provincial or Central Government. Sectoral programmes focus on particular sectors such as energy, farming and education, whereas regional programs are cross-cutting within the region covering matters such as transportation systems, electricity systems etc. MHPP projects are part of sectoral and regional development programmes.

Despite accelerated efforts from Central Government to develop villages, data in 2023 shows there are 50% of a total of 74,420 villages in Indonesia are still in the developing stage,[10] including 5,75% of villages in the 'very left behind' and 16,46% in the 'left behind' categories.[11]

There are many factors that hinder villages from become 'advanced' and even 'independent', ranging from the capacity of village leadership and its governance in managing development projects and their finances, to the capacity of the communities themselves. As discussed earlier, developing rural communities can be the object of development or the subject of development. They become the object of development when they are underdeveloped and lack knowledge and skills for their own self-development. Meanwhile, as the subject of development, rural communities who acquire the capacity to do so, can become the driving agent in development for their villages. In practice, often the ideas for development projects come from Government or other parties who tend to treat communities as the object of their policies. When treated as objects and their capacity remains undeveloped, it is often the case that villages tend to become even more dependent on Government.

Understanding the characteristics of rural communities is important in designing strategies which gain support for development. Rural villages are of smaller community sizes than in urban settings, with lower population densities.

Because most of the land is used for agriculture, rural populations need to be able to support their basic needs through their work and have enough surplus agricultural output to be able to sustain their communities. Their economies heavily rely on agriculture and collective enterprise. Rural communities are essentially social systems characterised by a social relationship based on a need to fulfil needs, habits and feelings. They consist of individuals, interconnected units and interdependencies such as family, education, economy, and religion, which together constitute community life. In rural communities, relationships have an organic structure with a low level of labour division, but high levels of collective consciousness. With this collective awareness, the ties among them are strong and this tends to generate similarity, conformity and uniformity.

Rural communities are organised into several groups. First, as mandated by the Government, to support village life and to provide a better community service, they are grouped into several neighbourhoods. Thus, within villages, there can be clusters of households, usually called *dusun* (hamlets), and each of these has a leader. There is no official Government representation operating at hamlet level; however, hamlets are grouped together in a village, where there is an official level of Government. Second, to empower women in improving community's welfare, there are women's groups, again as mandated by Government. Third, communities are also grouped according to their interests, such as farming groups and sewing groups. In addition, to discuss and organise village activities, there is a main forum called *Kelompok Kerja Lembaga Pemberdayaan Masyarakat Dusun/KKLPMD* (Working Group of Hamlet's Community Empowerment). This forum is held every 35 days and is attended by household heads most of whom are men, the representatives of community organisations, other community figures, such as religious and custom leaders. *Musrenbang,* referred to earlier, and which is for discussing development project plans, including MHPP, is conducted within this forum.

Further, social stratification in the village indicates vertical structuring, which positions groups in a hierarchical order. In the context of biosocial structure, i.e. structure related to such factors as gender and age, men in rural communities have a higher social standing than women. This is because women are more numerous than men and social norms position women as second-class community members. Older people occupy a higher social level than the young because of the experience associated with traditional livelihoods, such as agriculture.[12] Agricultural land is a factor because livelihoods in villages are entirely dependent on it. People with the right to use, cultivate, exploit and sell land have a high position in local society, indeed, this group is the most influential, particularly as they often include the founders of the village and their descendants. They are the people who form the core of the village governance structure. They have the right to speak, including in village meetings and decision-making processes.

In terms of cultural characteristics, a number of beliefs and norms characterise rural communities. Ethnic belief is based on kinship relations, local community, religious cosmology, and local traditions. 'Togetherness', which leads to a sense of shared destiny, locality, and fraternity is strong. In Rejeki's study[13] conducted on a village community in Java, it was found that the main point of social relations was to create a harmonious life, bringing inner peace and balance. This is manifested in acts of mutual help, deliberation, and harmonious living. Reciprocity is a key element of village value systems, i.e. the obligation to pay or reciprocate to others equivalent to that given by others to oneself. In the context of rural communities, the full life cycle is lived in reciprocity, from birth to death.

Value systems and local wisdom serve as social capital, or social investment to achieve goals and this emphasises community and social cohesion as the foundation of development. Local wisdom deals with most essential aspects of rural life, including food security, water resource conservation, natural resource utilisation, settlement, clothing, social interactions, disaster anticipation, social conflict and poverty. It is constructed, developed and fiercely defended by members of the village community.

Attention to these social and cultural elements of rural development is in line with the view that village development needs to put people first as the subject of development. The essence of this idea is that for development projects to be successful, these human factors should take precedence. This was a driving factor in the way the project team undertook its research and it is to this that we turn next.

Overall approach to the project

Theoretically the study used grounded thinking: we wanted to look at what was happening as we undertook our fieldwork and try to make sense of it after reflecting on what we found. Grounded thinking facilitates investigating, recording and interpreting the way communities interpret and make sense of their experiences and the world in which they live and then abstracting this into theoretical statements that fit the phenomenon under study. In our case, this has led to the construction of a new model of community engagement.

In line with grounded thinking, case study was selected as our methodology. Through case study, we were able to carry out a thorough analysis of how Government-led community engagement was undertaken in three hamlets in three different villages who were at different stages of adopting an MHPP. By spending considerable time with them, we were able to study them in their particular rural setting, comprehend engagement from the participants' points of view, note the many different factors in play and pay attention to how those factors relate to each other.

This case was chosen for three reasons. First, MHPP projects are a whole-community technology that requires collective participation to maintain its sustainability. Government therefore needs to consider such aspects as (a) identifying community members appropriate in decision-making; (b) building trust in the technology through village leaders or other influential community members; (c) focusing on community energy needs; (d) ensuring a level of community participation to ensure community ownership of the plant and (e) building a reliable institutional framework to ensure a successful and long-term sustainable renewable energy programme.

Second, MHPP takes at least two years to progress through five different stages to completion, i.e. pre-initiation, initiation, adoption, transition and sustainability. Each stage requires different approaches to engagement, which is why the three hamlets in the case study were chosen. Each one had reached different stages of completion, namely pre-initiation, adoption and sustainability. This allowed the research to examine the full life-cycle of MHPP engagement, capture the unique experiences of each hamlet along with community opinions about how it could be improved along with their ambitions for the future, while also looking for commonalities of experience and responses among them. It was not necessary to choose hamlets at every stage of development because the development cycle was fully covered by researching these three. However, to ensure memories of each part of the development cycle were fresh, it was decided that this 'staged' approach would be appropriate. We needed to be parsimonious in project budget and time and the results obtained were sufficient to be confident in making the recommendations we have. As the results will show, experiences were broadly similar and there was consensus on how the process could be improved.

Third, case study was chosen because it provided opportunities to understand how socio-cultural context contributes to community engagement and development in a non-Western country. As discussed in Chapter 2, it is important to acknowledge how indigenous knowledge systems support Government and other organisations in their understanding of problems and to generate solutions that are meaningful to rural communities.

Having provided the context of our project and a brief introduction to our approach, the next chapter gives detailed explanations on how the research was undertaken.

Notes

1 Ministry of Environment and Forestry (2021). Indonesia long-term strategy for low carbon and climate resilience 2050. Available at https://unfccc.int/sites/default/files/resource/Indonesia_LTS-LCCR_2021.pdf

2 Ardiansyah, H. (2022). Hydropower technology: Potential, challenges, and the future. In: H. Ardiansyah & P. Ekadewi, (eds.) *Indonesia post-pandemic outlook: Strategy towards net-zero emissions by 2060 from the renewables and carbon-neutral energy perspectives* (pp.89–107). BRIN Publishing: Jakarta.

3 Ministry of Energy and Mineral Resources of Indonesia 2020. *Indonesia Energy Outlook 2019*. National Energy Council: Jakarta

4 Erinofiardi, G.P., Date, A., Akbarzadeh, A., Bismantolo, P., Suryono, A. F., Mainil, A. K. & Nuramal, A. (2017). A review On micro hydropower in Indonesia. *Energy Procedia*, 110, 316–321; Rospriandana, N., Burke, P. J., Suryani, A., Mubarok, M. H. & Pangestu, M. A. (2023). Over a century of small hydropower projects in Indonesia: A historical review. *Energy, Sustainability and Society*, 13, 30.

5 Murni, S., Whale, J., Urmee, T., Davis, J. & Harries, D. (2012). The role of micro hydro power systems in remote rural electrification: A case study in The Bawan Valley, Borneo. *Energy Procedia*, 49, 189–196.

6 Cannon, M., Thorpe, J. & Emili, S. (2020). *IBEKA: community-owned and managed mini grids in Indonesia*. Institute of Development Studies UK (IDS): Brighton.

7 Parahita, G.D. (2018). Shifts and challenges of communication for sustainable development in Indonesia. In: K. Prasad (ed.) *Communication, culture and ecology, rethinking sustainable development in Asia*. pp.155–172. Springer: Singapore.

8 Tambunan, T.T H. (2012). Indonesia: Building an inclusive development mode. In: Y. Zhang, F. Kimura & S. Oum (eds.) *Moving toward a new development model for East Asia- The role of domestic policy and regional cooperation* (pp.223–254). ERIA: Jakarta.

9 Sindre, G. M. (2012). Civic engagement and democracy in post-Suharto Indonesia: A review of Musrenbang, the kecamatan development programme and labour organising. *Power Conflict and Democracy Journal*, 4(1-2), 1–40.

10 There are five categories in the Development Village Index: independent village, advanced village, developing villages, left behind village and very left behind village.

11 The Directorate General of Village and Rural Development (2023). Building village index [Online]. Available: https://idm.kemendesa.go.id

12 Ratriyana, I.N., Setiawan, L.D. & Yudarwati, G.A. (2021). Development communication for youth empowerment in Indonesia's renewable energy projects. *Asian Journal of Communication*, 32(4), 290–308.

13 Rejeki, N. S. (2007). Perbedaan budaya dan adaptasi antarbudaya dalam relasi kemitraan inti-plasma. *Jurnal Ilmu Komunikasi*, 4(2), 145–166.

4 How the research was undertaken

Having outlined in Chapter 3 the overall approach to researching Government-led community engagement on MHPP in three rural hamlets in Indonesia, we now detail how the work was undertaken.

It is important to state that full ethical approval was sought and given by the University of Huddersfield before beginning the research project.[1] Huddersfield was the British Council Newton Fund Institutional Links[1] research grant holder. The research team were very aware that they were dealing with communities whose norms and values were different from their own and should be respected and upheld. Their knowledge and willing cooperation were vital.

Analysis of Government documents and policies

Prior to the study in the three hamlets commencing, the research team undertook a number of activities to ensure they were well informed about Government policies and project implementation and communication practices:

- a review of Government policies, papers and documents relevant to the project, including documentation on renewable energy, the Government strategic development plan for energy and national governance policy;
- fact-finding interviews with central Government officials to obtain a clear understanding of policy and practice on renewable energy initiatives;
- fact-finding interviews with local authority officials, i.e. leaders of districts and villages, to verify information on MHPP ownership status and the installation process from pre-initiation to the sustainability stage.

The data collected from these sources revealed that MHPP project planning and implementation at the province level is the responsibility of the Government agency Department of Public Works, Housing, Energy, and Mineral Resources (*Dinas Pekerjaan Umum, Perumahan, Energi dan Sumber Daya Mineral*/PUPESDM).

DOI: 10.4324/9781003507444-4

The stages of the MHPP project lifecycle

The research team also discovered that there are five distinct stages to the MHPP projects, which it calls the MHPP project lifecycle. This cycle describes the agreed process for MHPP installation and ownership of the plant.

- Stage 1: *pre-initiation*. Here, PUPESDM in conjunction with City/Regency and District level Government appoints a consultant to undertake a feasibility study (FS) for a particular hamlet. Based on secondary data alone, an initial report provides a socio-economic assessment of potential and decides where a plant should be located. If Government approves the initial report, plant design and budget are proposed in a final report. At this stage the project is agreed or abandoned. During the FS, the community is not involved, and indeed may never know that an FS was undertaken in their hamlet. If the outcome is positive, a license to operate is granted and the community are informed through *socialisation* (see Chapter 5 for more detail on this).
- Stage 2: *initiation*. This is when PUPESDM initiates the installation of the MHPP. They appoint a building contractor as project manager, and the MHPP is built with community support in the form of volunteer labour and paid labour, food for the construction workers and such like. Concurrently, PUPESDM selects three to five volunteers from the community and trains them so that they can maintain the MHPP on a daily basis, and this includes undertaking simple repairs.
- Stage 3: *adoption*. At this stage, the community tries out and adopts the MHPP, with PUPESDM support and supervision. The community learns to operate and use the plant. Initially, energy generated from the MHPP is used mostly for street and domestic lighting and other basic uses, including charging electrical devices such as mobile phones. The community begins to expand its ambitions for energy use now that they have a reliable and more plentiful resource, particularly to support economic activity. At this stage, PUPESDM still has responsibility for the overall maintenance of the MHPP and will monitor its use and performance to ensure it is adequate for the community.
- Stage 4: *transition*. Here, the community prepares to manage the MHPP so that they can run it independently of Government. During the transition stage, the community must create an MHPP Organisation and this needs to operate independently for at least three years before the community takes over the plant. At the end of this stage, the Government hands over responsibility for the plant and its operations (including its financial management) to the MHPP Organisation.
- Stage 5: *sustainability*. Communities exploit MHPP usage and strengthen community ownership so that its long-term sustainability and developing

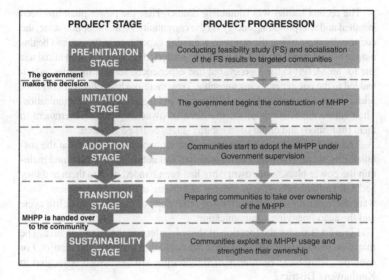

Figure 4.1 The five stages of the MHPP project lifecycle[2]

use are assured. The community has self-determination in making decisions about the MHPP.

Figure 4.1 summarises this process.

The three hamlets

Kulon Progo Regency was chosen as the site for the field research after consultation with province Government. This Regency is considered as having good examples of community-based renewable energy projects and had three hamlets in three separate villages that were at different stages of adopting an MHPP. It was also in a rural area easily accessible to the group undertaking the research, which was important given the amount of time that was to be spent with them.

The first hamlet, Kalisonggo Hamlet, was at the pre-initiation stage. Micro-hydro power had not been introduced, but the Government had conducted an FS although the community was not aware of this. It was important to conduct research with this community and at this stage in order to understand perceptions about micro-hydro power from unaware communities. The research team also wanted to ask the community how they saw a future with a constant electricity supply and how they wished to be communicated with if an FS identified their hamlet as being suitable for an MHPP installation.

The second hamlet was Blumbang Hamlet. Here the power plant had been installed and was providing energy for the community. At this adoption stage, the community were trying the equipment, gaining experience in its use, and beginning to exploit its potential. This hamlet was selected because it was an initial test site for an MHPP in the regency, but had experienced some difficulties, which had led to the equipment being unusable. They therefore had reflective insight of initial installation and subsequent difficulties and the associated communication. Their future expectations of the transition of ownership from Government to them (transition) and of the sustainability stages could be captured.

The third hamlet was Kedungrong Hamlet, which was already at the sustainability stage. Here, the community had full authority to exploit and maintain the power plant, since ownership had been handed over to them and they had full responsibility for its current and future use and development. They were therefore able to offer informed reflections of the full project life cycle and the accompanying communication.

Figure 4.2 shows the location of these hamlets on the island of Java. The map also shows the location of each hamlet within a village and district. For example, Blumbang Hamlet is in Banjararum village, which is located in Kalibawang District.

How the research was undertaken

To obtain data about the hamlets' experience of how Government communicated with them on their MHPP, all stages of the MHPP project lifecycle had to be investigated, with a particular emphasis on how community engagement was undertaken. The research team considered and rejected several methods for data collection in the hamlets including individual and convened group interviews, questionnaires, and non-participatory observation. The team were cautious about using Western research techniques, which as explained in Chapter 3, are alien to the experience and culture of rural communities and might be regarded as threatening.

We sought a rigorous approach that honoured and capitalised on familiar routines and would fit in with cultural norms more readily. We also wanted a method that maximised opportunities to hear first-hand experiences and mined the rich sources of knowledge and understanding within these hamlets. A conversation-based approach was deemed most appropriate and a deliberative method was chosen. This satisfied the data collection requirements while encouraging exploration, discovery, ownership and empowerment.

The deliberative method is in sympathy with the culture of rural communities, who have strong personal and cultural bonds, and who meet frequently to discuss matters that relate to them, as explained in Chapter 3. Within the deliberative suite of techniques,[4] Appreciative Inquiry was determined to be most suitable. This technique is non-confrontational and helps communities

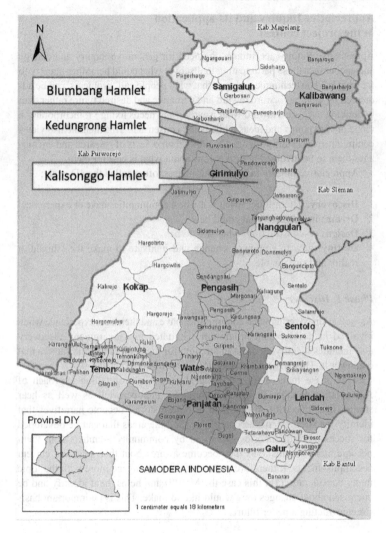

Figure 4.2 The location of the three hamlets in Java[3]

discover their best experiences and the most appropriate way to prepare for, participate in and exploit the opportunities offered by their MHPP. Appreciative Inquiry is essentially how communities conduct their hamlet business: the researchers' task was to frame and capture what was happening. The study found that the four phases of Appreciative Inquiry, as described below, were applicable to each of the five stages of project development.

Appreciative Inquiry and its application in the project context

Appreciative Inquiry accentuates the need for generative inquiry and change and encourages those participating to discover what could be, rather than try to fix what is.[5] The technique suggests that what people call 'problems' can be addressed by looking forward toward an alternative and desired future rather than by looking backward toward what is wrong and needs fixing.[6] It incorporates a range of viewpoints and ideas while being consensual. This method also views communities as actors with agency rather than objects of research and encourages them to be involved in discussions about what is best for them.

Appreciative Inquiry involves four phases, often called the 4D cycle:

1 **Discovery:** determining 'what is the best communities have or experience'
2 **Dream:** imagining 'what could be'
3 **Design:** co-constructing 'what should be'
4 **Destiny:** how to empower, change and innovate to make the 'should' a reality and sustainable.

Phase 1: Discovery

As well as discovering what communities have and their best experience when involved in development programmes initiated by Government, discovery also includes identifying areas of strength for the community and factors that empower it. This is the data collection phase of the 4D cycle.

This phase focused on gathering stories. The storytelling approach of Appreciative Inquiry, in which community members tell as well as hear stories, is in line with an oral culture. These stories become narratives that identify the strengths of the community and the areas that can be developed for success. Positive stories expressed by community members help them become more optimistic as they become aware about their past and current accomplishments. It therefore motivates them to engage more with the topic under consideration (in this case the MHPP) and helps them identify and be energised about changes they would like to make. This is an important basis for constructing a better future.

Phase 2: Dream

The dream phase focuses on creating a vision of the future, but not its actual design or implementation. The community is encouraged to dream or create a vision of what they want to be or what the hamlet could be. This means identifying new possibilities for how the community might function and deliver the development project. The use of positive questions in the discovery phase focuses on the possible rather than the problems they have.

Phase 3: Design

Design requires translating the vision into a plan of action. It designs the social, administrative, and other infrastructure and processes that are needed to make the vision a reality. This includes defining and designing the social norms, values, policies, methods, processes and procedures to realise the vision. Three main questions guide these discussions: what, who and how to realise the vision.

Phase 4: Destiny/Delivery

The destiny phase brings to life the vision the community has imagined and planned. It is both the conclusion of the Discovery, Dream and Design phases and the beginning of an ongoing commitment to achieve future goals.

The research team were aware that Appreciative Inquiry originated and is used in Western cultures, so they made adjustments to make it appropriate to the Indonesian rural context.

First, the research was conducted in Bahasa, the local language. Second, as much as possible, researchers used existing community group structures such as those mandated by Government to undertake their data collection. MHPP are discussed as a matter of course in these settings, because they are so central to hamlet and village social and economic life. This gave a 'natural' opportunity to conduct what were effectively focus group discussions (FGDs). However, the participants of these FGDs were not selected, and neither were the groups conducted in conformity with formal protocols for FGDs, instead, they were undertaken with whoever was in attendance at the meetings and as discursive conversations.

These FGDs were scheduled by the hamlets themselves and undertaken in informal settings. While the research team recognised that there might be issues raised about the validity of the composition of the FGDs, the appreciative philosophy allows for flexibility as the context demands. The team judged that this adaption would obtain the best quality and quantity of data from the community and their experience was that hamlet communities appeared to speak with them freely, openly and at some length.

Third, the individual phases of Appreciative Inquiry were tailored to the local context as follows:

Discover. How to gather the stories was a key question. In Indonesian culture individual appreciation becomes collective appreciation, individual will evolves into group will, and individual vision becomes a cooperative or shared vision for the community. From their stories, communities created "positive maps" that showed their hopes, needs, strengths, relationships, affiliations, and other assets in their communities.

Well-constructed questions lead to constructive storytelling from the participants, as well as reflection and learning from their positive past experiences. Great care was taken in ensuring the questions were non-confrontational as well as information-gathering. Some examples of questions are:

- Tell us about your past experiences living in this hamlet. What are the best experiences you have had? Can you tell us a story about a particular time when you and the community were working at your best?
- What do you think has made this hamlet become what it is now?
- What best practices does this hamlet have? What community values and/or local customs support them?
- Tell us about your experience of a Government development project. Can you remember a time when you and the community participated in such a project? What made the development project possible? What did the community do to support the project? What other factors made the project possible/successful?

Dream. Appreciative Inquiry facilitators organised community meetings and discussions in ways that encouraged dreaming. As the vision was developed, it was shared using whatever creative methods that are acceptable to the local community, such as visual images, traditional dance or drama to describe future dreams. In this study, hamlet dreams were drawn as a process diagram. Some example questions to stimulate dreaming included:

- What do we want our hamlet to be in the future?
- What opportunities can we take to have a better future?
- What kind of businesses do we want for our hamlet and wider village? Family? What else we want to develop in our village?

Design. In rural collective communities, it is usual that leaders or those who they believe understand the topic best, develop the design. The critical point here is that all parts of the community, including local leaders, are represented in the design phase.

Destiny. Communities were invited to a free discussion about planning and commitment during this phase. They discussed what they could and would do to contribute to the realisation of their dreams and, because of their culture, their conclusions committed them to act so that a jointly envisioned future could be realised.

The use and adaption of Appreciative Inquiry to local conditions was not just a pragmatic decision to obtain the best possible data, but also was an ethical one which sought to respect and honour local customs and culture.

Data collection

There was a total of 15 FGDs conducted in the three hamlets. The groups involved are shown in Table 4.1.

In addition to the FGDs, there were individual unstructured and conversational interviews with the leaders of each of the three hamlets. These were to gain initial information about the hamlet, including community structure, culture and the key actors that the research team should engage with, as well as information about development projects including MHPP. Interviews with hamlet leaders were important: in collective cultures approval and support from leaders is essential to gain community support and participation. The hamlet leaders were also able to help identify which community groups could most usefully participate in the research. In addition, they became the liaison person between the research team and their communities. Through these leaders, the research team had unhindered access to community groups.

An additional individual interview was carried out in Blumbang Hamlet, which was at the adoption stage, with one of the MHPP technicians in order to understand technical issues and Government support in solving problems with the equipment. In Kedungrong Hamlet, which was at the sustainability stage, interviews were also conducted with representatives of the MHPP Organisation (which is responsible for the operation of the plant and includes volunteers who have been trained by the Government to run the plant) and the pioneers (community member who were chosen by the hamlet leader to champion the use of MHPP and to support home industries). The interviews with the MHPP Organisation and pioneers were to capture their experiences in exploiting the electrical power to date and the accompanying communication

Table 4.1 Number and composition of focus group discussion groups

Hamlet	Focus group discussion (FGD)
Kalisonggo Hamlet	• 2 FGDs with household leaders groups, i.e. *rukun tetangga* or neighbourhood groups (only one female in each group)
	• 2 FGDs with female *dasawisma groups*
	• 1 FGD with youth group
Blumbang Hamlet	• 1 FGDs with household leaders groups, i.e. *rukun tetangga* or neighbourhood groups (consisted of 4 female and 19 male participants)
	• 1 FGD with female group (PKK)
	• 1 FGD with youth group
Kedungrong Hamlet	• 3 FGDs with household leaders groups, i.e. *rukun tetangga* or neighbourhood groups (all of them male)
	• 3 FGDs with female *dasawisma groups*
	• 1 FGD with female
TOTAL	15 FGDs

process and to hear from them how these could be improved to enable them to capitalise further on the MHPP benefits.

The data collection process followed four steps:

1 Initiation

    There were two main parts in this step: firstly, to introduce the project and the research team to the hamlet leaders. Secondly, to collect initial information about the hamlet to map stakeholders involved in the MHPP and to map community groups and forums in which to conduct the FGDs.

2 Community consent and support

    After gaining permission from the hamlet leaders, the team was invited by them to their main hamlet's forum and introduced to the household representatives and community group leaders. The team explained the project and the timeframe and most importantly asked for consent and participation from the community. This step was important, not only to comply with University ethics requirements, but to gain acceptance and build trust as well as to avoid misinterpretation and suspicion from the community who are wary of people from outside their immediate circle.

3 Conducting the FGDs and individual interviews

    In the third step, the research team arranged schedules for FGDs with support from the head of the hamlet who informed the researchers of the availability of each community group (Figure 4.3).

    Each FGD followed the four phases of the Appreciative Inquiry cycle, as described above. In each phase, communities discussed the technical, management, and life-enhancing opportunities associated with the MHPP installation. They also discussed the accompanying communication. In the first phase, i.e. discovery, communities were asked to articulate their best experiences of development projects, including the installation of their MHPP. In the second phase, i.e. dream, communities were encouraged to imagine their ideal future when they own and can fully exploit the MHPP for their benefit. This included their reasonable expectations of how things could be managed and operated, and their imaginings about an ideal future that might or might not be realisable. Ideas and images that came out of the dream phase became agenda items for the next step, the design phase. Finally, in the delivery phase they were encouraged to state intended actions to realise their plan and crucially, they were asked what support was needed to convert this into reality.

    The individual interviews were also conducted within the same timeframe. Interviews and FGDs were recorded and transcribed with community consent.

4 Checking the data collection process

    To check its scope and to wrap up the data collection process, the research team mapped the community groups involved to make sure all were

Figure 4.3 Women's group meeting in Kalisonggo Hamlet (photograph used with participants' permission)

represented. The data transcribed from FGDs and interviews were analysed to identify findings, themes and patterns from each hamlet in order to compare similarities and differences.

In sum, the mix of secondary and primary data, along with a research approach, methodology and methods carefully identified and adapted to satisfy both the need for rigour and the particular cultural requirements of the communities under investigation, meant the research team where able to obtain rich data.

Having outlined the methodology, methods and process for data collection, the next chapter provides an introduction for the case studies and the three detailed cases.

Notes

1 As recognised in the Acknowledgements, the research underpinning this project was funded by British Council Newton Fund Institutional Links Grant ID 217488952 - Indonesia.

2 Yudarwati, G. A. & Gregory, A. (2022). Improving government communication and empowering rural communities: Combining public relations and development communication approaches. *Public Relations Review*, 48(3). Article 102200.

3 Map taken from website of Department of Public Works, Indonesia, Available at https://dpu.kulonprogokab.go.id/detil/297/pengelolaan-irigasi-kabupaten-kulon-progo%0A

4 Curato, N., Niemeyer, S. & Dryzek, J. (2013). Appreciative and contestatory inquiry in deliberative forums: Can group hugs be dangerous? *Critical Policy Studies*, 7(1), 1–17.

5 Cooperrider, D. L., Whitney, D. K. & Stavros, J. M. (2008). *Appreciative inquiry handbook : for leaders of change* (2nd ed.). Berrett-Koehler Publisher: San Francisco; Bushe, G. R. (2013). Appreciative inquiry. In E. H. Kessler (ed.) *Encyclopedia of management theory*, (pp. 1–5). Sage: California.
6 Crestani, I. (2015). Appreciative inquiry as a shadow process in communicating change. *Fusion*, 7(3), 220–233.

5 Discovering community communication preferences and needs

This Chapter covers the three hamlet case studies in turn and to aid understanding of key points, summaries for each are provided in tabular form.

Kalisonggo Hamlet

Kalisonggo Hamlet is located in Pendoworejo Village, Girimulyo District, Kulon Progo Regency. Its population of 219 people live in 69 households. An FS was conducted in Kalisonggo in 2016 by PUPESDM.

This hamlet case study describes what happened in the pre-initiation stage of the MHPP project and the communication process experienced by the community. We also researched the community's hopes and ambitions if the MHPP project were to be initiated and therefore the data collected reflects the community's aspirations for all stages of the MHPP project cycle, i.e. pre-initiation, initiation, adoption, transition and sustainability. Actors, communication content and channels are described.

Pre-initiation stage

In the pre-initiation stage, the community was neither informed nor involved in any of the FS activities. However, when asked by the research team, the community expressed their willingness to share their knowledge and assist the Government appointed consultant, irrespective of whether the MHPP would be installed in their hamlet or not.

The final results of the FS were presented by the consultant to PUPESDM and local authorities at Regency, District, and Village levels, to gain feedback from areas that were impacted by the project not proceeding. The *socialisation* process in the community, however, was not undertaken, since PUPSEDM had decided not to build an MHPP in Kalisonggo. Socialisation consists of the hamlet leader being told that an MHPP would be installed in their locality, and then, at a meeting called by the hamlet leader, the Government, represented by a PUPESDM official, tells the hamlet community about the development, its benefits and how the installation will take place. Feedback is also solicited as

DOI: 10.4324/9781003507444-5

part of the formal project process. A request for volunteers to assist with the installation is also made at this stage. Usually there is just one socialisation meeting and its purpose is very clearly to 'tell and sell': the decision to install the MHPP has been made without community involvement. The socialisation is conducted in the KKLPMD, which is the main decision-making forum in the hamlet. (A fuller explanation of how the socialisation process was undertaken in Blumbang Hamlet is given below.)

Community's views about communication on an approved MHPP development project

Pre-initiation stage

During the pre-initiation stage, the community expected to be informed about and involved in FS activities. The hamlet leader also hoped to be invited by PUPESDM to attend the FS results presentation meeting to the Provincial Government so that he could gain information and provide feedback to the community (Figure 5.1). The community ideally wanted information directly from PUPESDM as the initiator of the project, not just from the consultant, with whom

Figure 5.1 Feasibility study in progress in Kalisonggo Hamlet (photograph used with participant's permission)

they had had informal contact during his survey visits. Their experience of communication in other development projects is usually multistep, i.e. not directly from the initiator to the hamlet when it is from Government at the Province or Regency level, but via the District and Village. The implication of this is that those people who eventually communicate with hamlets often lack important information, for example, if successful, how implementation will be undertaken, the budget available and the timeframe for implementation. The expectation of hamlets for MHPP is that PUPESDM should share information directly with all community groups through community meetings.

Initiation stage

In the initiation stage, the hamlet wanted the whole community, including women to participate in discussions about the installation of the plant so that they too could realise their dreams for MHPP. Based on their experience of other projects, discussion of proposals and implementation of projects is at the hamlet elite level and other residents, including women and young people, are treated merely as recipients of decisions.

Adoption stage

In Kalisonggo, the community asserted that they rarely reject any Government development projects. They were clear that if they had been awarded a MHPP they would need explicit and detailed information about how to access and operate the MHPP, as well as a full explanation of the benefits they would gain from it. In addition, accessible, credible information which would provide the support and information needed during the adoption stage is also expected.

Transition stage

In this hamlet they would like the youth group (Karang Taruna) with all their ideas and enthusiasm to participate in managing their MHPP and in setting up its management organisation. Karang Taruna has a desire to undertake management responsibilities – it gives them status and, because they can see that they can shape their own future, a reason to stay in the hamlet: the draw of towns and cities is strong because of employment and social opportunities. The hamlet believed these young people could become the driving force for development when working together with the senior figures and elite of the hamlet.

The community also wanted to develop their overall capabilities, for example, technical knowledge and skills so that they could take over competently and confidently when the MHPP was handed to community. They were willing to take responsibility for ownership.

Table 5.1 Findings and observations about Kalisonggo Hamlet

Stage	Issue	Aspiration
Pre-initiation	• Information from local Government to community • Extended socialisation	• Community wants to know about the pre-initiation stage • Direct communication from initiator (PUPESDM) to community through hamlet meetings • Recommendation: inform the community about the FS result, even if it is not to go ahead
Initiation	Installation	All community groups (including women and youth) to be involved in project implementation
Adoption	Adequate information about MHPP operations	• The community needs clear and detailed information about how to access and operate the MHPP, as well as the benefits they will gain from it. • They also want ongoing, accessible and credible sources to provide information needed by the community
Transition	Technical Management	Training to develop capability • Management training • Collaboration between youth and the elite of the hamlet
Sustainability	Usage	Alternative energy for households and to support economic activities

Sustainability stage

In the sustainability stage, the community aspired to make use of MHPP to cut the cost of their state electricity bills and to exploit economic potential. Various community groups had aspirations, for example, young mothers wanted to grow home industries such as sewing and carpentry, and the farmers group expected that electricity could be used to develop chicken farming and other agricultural businesses. In the community's view, the MHPP is an alternative, extended and more reliable source of electrical energy that has economic benefits. Their hope is that one day the MHPP will be installed, become their main source of electrical energy and that they will be able to exploit it to the full.

Table 5.1 presents a summary of the community's aspirations

Blumbang Hamlet

Blumbang Hamlet is located in Banjararum Village, Kalibawang District, Kulon Progo Regency, Yogyakarta Province. MHPP development in Blumbang began in 2013 after the installation in Kedungrong Hamlet was completed. The location of both hamlets is close even though they are in different administrative local Government areas. To meet the needs of Blum-bang Hamlet, which has 125 households, two MHPP turbines were built with an engine capacity of 30,000 kWh each. Unfortunately, only one turbine is able to run at any one time.

The construction of electricity networks for households and street lighting began in 2015, but it was not until mid-2017 that the MHPP was able to support the whole hamlet's electricity needs. At the time of the research, the MHPP was in the adoption stage, under the supervision and responsibility of PUPESDM, who monitor performance before it is handed over to the community.

For this case study, we describe what happened in the pre-initiation, initia-tion and adoption stages, including the communication processes experienced by the community and the actors, messages/content, and channels involved. We also describe community's future expectations when the MHPP project is given over to them and beyond (transition and sustainability stages).

Pre-initiation stage

Blumbang and Kedungrong Hamlets were included in the same FS conducted in 2011, and both were part of the MHPP proposal for Kedungrong (with Blumbang being described as Kedungrong 2). No one from the community in Blumbang was involved in the FS; indeed, it was regarded as a continuation of the Kedungrong programme.

The Blumbang community were first informed of their MHPP during the socialisation process in October 2012 at a hamlet meeting. As for Kalisonggo, there were two parts to the communication. First, PUPESM asked the head of hamlet to coordinate the socialisation meeting for Blumbang community representatives. Second, the socialisation meeting with Blumbang commu-nity representatives whose houses were closest to the MHPP facility, i.e. 55 households, who were due to be connected to the MHPP electricity supply. Budget limitations did not allow the whole hamlet of 125 households to be connected initially. Socialisation was undertaken by speakers from PU-PESDM, the consultant, the construction contractor and village officers of Banjararum Village within whose jurisdiction the hamlet lies. The meeting was attended by the leaders of each of the 55 households. As required in the project process, the community was informed that an MHPP would be in-stalled and feedback requested, although in reality, information-giving rather than opinion and local knowledge input was the focus. As part of the formal project procedure, community feedback is to be included in a report on the socialisation process, which must be attached to two documents (Environ-mental Management Effort and Environmental Monitoring Effort), which shows both the impacts of the MHPP on the environment and the proposed solution to manage these impacts. Once these documents are submitted and approved, the MHPP project can be initiated.

The community's response during and after socialisation was positive. Even though they did not have any details about the MHPP, they accepted the idea of a development that could enhance their community and quality of life. They too perceived MHPP as an alternative source of electricity to the national grid, which they regarded as being expensive and unreliable.

Initiation stage

After the MHPP was approved by the Provincial Government, installation was initiated in 2013, with the community being informed about the project plan (developed by PUPESDM) in order to obtain their support. At the same time, three technicians were recruited from the community. During the installation stage, these technicians received communication and training from PUPESDM, the consultant, and the construction contractor. Some community members were also involved by assisting in construction and others, for example, women, supported by preparing food for the workers as part of *gotong royong* (collective mutual help). However, due to landslides and bad weather conditions, the turbines did not function. To be able to repair the MHPP, the contractor had to inform the PUPESDM so that a funding request could be included in their annual budget plan, a bureaucratic and extended process. The repair funding was finally covered in the 2014 and 2015 budget plans.

The installation in Blumbang consisted of two turbines providing 55 households with an electricity network and street lighting. The fact that the budget did not allow for all households to be connected was not communicated to the whole community. However, given the turbines did not work for approximately two years, there was disillusionment about the potential of the MHPP throughout the community.

Adoption stage

It was not until the middle of 2017 that the MHPP was fully operational and then only for the 55 households. Communication issues during this transition stage can be categorised under three headings: 1) technology related, 2) MHPP management and 3) benefits and utilisation.

1) Technology-related communication issues

There were two types of issues here: *routine* and *non-routine* communication. First, routine communication between technicians and PUPESDM during the trial period is largely about two things:

- monitoring and maintaining the MHPP to ensure it works properly before being handed over to the community,
- routine issues such as the unstable electricity flow from the MHPP or the maintenance of the MHPP turbine.

The technicians had to report to the PUPESDM monthly and receive a monthly salary until the MHPP is handed over to the community.

Second, non-routine communication is mainly about MHPP mechanical problems. If this is considered small-scale, the technician can consult a dedicated MHPP consultant to obtain technical assistance. However, for larger-scale problems technicians need to inform the hamlet leader, who requests PUPESDM for technical support. PUPESDM will then ask a more experienced consultant to solve the problem. In these cases mobile phone, either using text or call services, has become the main channel of communication between the technicians and the consultant. For large-scale problems that require significant funding from the regency, PUPESDM must submit a proposal, which will then be included in the annual budget plan of the Regency.

This study found that often unstable electricity flow was caused by rubbish, which blocked the canal into the MHPP turbine. To overcome this problem, support from communities is needed:

- to help remove the rubbish, and
- to change behaviour to not throwing household waste into irrigation channels.

The technicians communicate with the head of hamlet to gain support for this.

2) MHPP Management Issues

Communities discussed issues relating to the management of their MHPP in the hamlet meeting and it was decided to assign the youth group to undertake the operational management of the MHPP: they planned to create a special division to manage the MHPP. At the same time, the general management of the MHPP such as issues of larger scale maintenance, community fees and which additional households will obtain electricity from the MHPP, was discussed in the hamlet meeting.

During the adoption period, the community explained that they enjoyed the economic benefit of the MHPP especially for lighting roads and houses. The use of MHPP decreased the cost of electricity, especially benefiting those who did not receive any Government subsidy. Other benefits were supporting home-based businesses such as laundry services, grocery shops, copying services and carpentry. Indeed, the benefits were regarded as so positive that some hamlet members who were not in the 55 households bought their own connection equipment, which allowed them access to the power generated.

3) MHPP Benefits and Utilisation

Information about benefits and how to utilise the MHPP were shared among family and community members. At the community level, information about the MHPP came from technicians, neighbours (the 55 households who were already connected) and from the neighbouring hamlet (Kedungrong) who had taken over ownership of their MHPP. The main channels for communication were face-to-face and *getok tular* (Word of Mouth). Even though they enthusiastically accepted the MHPP, they were still doubtful about using it to support their electronic devices because the voltage was unstable.

Community's views about communication on an approved MHPP development project

Transition stage

During the research the community was asked to articulate their aspirations for their MHPP during the transition stage. They wanted to have a better MHPP *management system*. They also had expectations about expanding usage to fully realise its *benefits*, more than just for reducing their electricity bills. They planned to collect a monthly fee from hamlet households to develop the infrastructure network so that more households could be connected.

There was also enthusiasm within the *karang taruna* group to take on the operational management of the MHPP even though they had not received technical training. They wanted to learn to be MHPP technicians and develop social and home industries such as creating a garden for social gatherings or eco-tourism. Generating more income was a prime motivator.

The farmers group were enthusiastic too. They built a collective cowshed, which was donated by Abdullah Gymnastiar Institutions and planned to use the MHPP to connect a pump to provide water. In addition, the hamlet leader's wife planned to use electricity to power cooking equipment, having provided training to help the women's group earn more income by selling food. However, the women were not so keen to develop this food business because they were content to be farmers. A key point here is that good communication around the potential of the MHPP can help to raise community aspirations beyond the here-and-now and subsistence levels of existence. Indeed, these raised aspirations are in line with the whole MHPP project objectives as developed by PUPESDM and driven by Government policy.

Sustainability stage

Despite having supervision from PUPESDM and realistic and realisable aspirations from the community, the hamlet did not expect that the MHPP would be handed over to them so quickly. The decision on the timing of the handover is based on how long the community has had an MHPP

Organisation (three years since it was set up), not on how prepared they are. The hamlet was dissatisfied with this because of their lack of technical skills, management knowledge and limited financial resources – no latitude in the timeline had been allowed for the fact that the turbines were not in operation for two years.

In addition, the incentive to own and fully exploit the MHPP only emerges when results can be seen, such as when they see that their neighbouring hamlet houses remain lit when there is a cut in national grid-supplied electricity.

A summary of the communication issues and observations emerging from the Blumbang case is as follows (Table 5.2):

Table 5.2 Findings and observations about Blumbang Hamlet

Stage	Discussion Point	Comment/Recommendation
Pre Initiation	• The Government initiated MHPP in Blumbang via an FS. • No community involvement. • The socialisation was to inform the head of hamlet, then continued to the households near the MHPP. • The information was only about the MHPP development plan. Insufficient information about the MHPP more broadly, i.e. maintenance budget and hand-over. • Those not connected to the plant were not informed.	• Government should develop a more comprehensive and grounded FS using primary data obtained from the community – they knew landslip was likely in the MHPP location chosen by the consultant. • Socialisation should be with all community groups • The community should be made aware of their responsibilities and eventual ownership of the plant. • The communication should involve all households, including those not to be connected.
Initiation	• The installation plan was developed by PUPESDM and community then informed to obtain support. • The community became an executor of installation plans. • Information was mainly about technical aspects and only with authority figures and technicians • Not all parts of the community were involved in discussions.	MHPP project installation plan should be developed and agreed by both PUPESDM and the community. Community becomes an empowered actor in the installation process.

(Continued)

Table 5.2 (Continued)

Stage	Discussion Point	Comment/Recommendation
Adoption	• Only 55 households connected to MHPP. • It is used for street lighting and to power household appliances • The unconnected households need to know what the future holds for them. • MHPP is still in the trial period, which is monitored by PUPESDM. • More households need to be informed about the transition arrangements so that they can be involved in decision-making and make a contribution to hamlet development.	• More structured communication to all parts of the community • Active involvement of community groups to explore needs and aspirations for MHPP. • Remind the community about future ownership of the MHPP, and agree on the process and practicalities of how to achieve it.
Transition	• The community has plans to develop the usage of MHPP, i.e. MHPP management organisation, tourism, home industry, agriculture, social spaces, etc. • To do this they need technical skills and management training.	• Inform community about future connection plans, encourage aspirations and involve all community groups. • Agree plan for future ownership. • Prepare the community for the future. Third-party assistance needed. • Identify capability training needs. Third-party assistance needed.
Sustainability	The community did not expect the MHPP to be handed over to the hamlet so quickly because of their lack of technical skills, management knowledge and limited financial resources.	Assumptions for the future • Community agrees hand over the procedure. • Training for MHPP operations and management has been completed • Third-party help to support has been started during trial phase • Identification of any economic sectors (such as eco-tourism, home industry, etc) that can be exploited has been conducted.

(*Continued*)

Table 5.2 (Continued)

Stage	Discussion Point	Comment/Recommendation
		RECOMMENDATION: to enable communities to exploit MHPP usage and to strengthen community ownership:
		• Involve communities through various forums to develop programmes and include them in village/hamlet development plans: short (annual programme), medium (5 years plan), and long (25 years plan) • Maintain communication with PUPESDM to obtain ongoing intelligence (for PUPESDM). Updates from PUPESDM on Government policy/support (for hamlet)

Kedungrong Hamlet

Kedungrong Hamlet is Purwosari Village, Girimulyo District and the MHPP has supported electricity needs since 2012. Kedungrong has 50 households, with most residents reliant on farming. Most of hamlet's young people live outside Kedungrong continuing their studies or working.

This case study describes what happens at all stages of MHPP projects with Kedungrong being the only hamlet in the research that had experienced all and the communication that accompanied them. This study captures their experiences, their reflections and expectations and identifies actors, messages/content and channels. A communication gap analysis leads to proposals for improvements.

Pre-initiation stage

In the case of Kedungrong, the community had previous experience with MHPP before the Government became involved. This came in 2010 from the social services provided by students from Gadjah Mada University, a public university in Yogyakarta. Students developed a small-scale micro hydro plant for this hamlet. The community was enthusiastic and supported the students' project, providing local materials, such as bamboo and labour for building a public lighting network. Although they had a very simple infrastructure, the community enjoyed the benefits of public lighting and this

Figure 5.2 MHPP water source and power plant in Kedungrong Hamlet

experience encouraged them to propose a full MHPP to PUPESDM, which then conducted an FS.

While conducting the FS, PUPESDM coordinated with the Serayu-Opak Board River Basin Management Organisation, which oversaw water management, and the Association of Water-Using Farmers (Figure 5.2). Both institutions have the authority to give or withhold permits for projects that may affect water and irrigation systems and they agreed to support the MHPP. PU-PESDM then applied to the Provincial Government for an operational license and project execution. The time and activity line covering the student project and the installation of the MHPP are given in Figure 5.3.

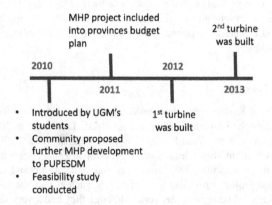

Figure 5.3 Time and activity line for installation of student micro-hydro plant and the full MHPP

PUPESDM initially envisaged the MHPP to serve Kedungrong Hamlet and two others nearby, Dukuh Hamlet and Duwet Hamlet. However, due to their geographical position and the topography of the area, this was not possible. Given the local culture, this created a feeling of discomfort among the inhabitants of Kedungrong because it might create discord with the other two hamlets.

Pre-initiation stage

PUPESDM conducted socialisation once, during a meeting at Kedungrong that was attended by local leaders representing Regency, District and Village levels. This meeting was also attended by coordinators of Kedungrong community groups, most of whom were men. The main message delivered by PUPESDM was the Government's plan to build the MHPP in Kedungrong and its benefits for the community. However, as with the other hamlets in this study, there was no discussion about the management and future of MHPP.

Initiation stage

Once the MHPP development was finally approved, PUPESDM informed the hamlet leader in order to gain support from the community. The first MHPP turbine was built in 2012 and was followed by the installation of another turbine in 2013 to add more power.

The installation of the MHPP involved community members: some were paid, including some who were without work at the time being given opportunities by PUPESDM. Others supported by preparing food or volunteering. While the installation was being undertaken, PUPESDM asked the hamlet leader to appoint three persons to undertake technical MHPP training. These three representatives were appointed by the hamlet based on their experience and background in mechanics. Further communication then came from PUPESDM to the head of Kedungrong and the technicians and this mainly concerned preparing the community for the installation of the MHPP.

The hamlet of Kedungrong perceived the MHPP as a Government project aimed at supporting their development, so they accepted it positively and dedicated effort into maintaining the plant. If there was any negative perception, it was mostly related to the unstable electricity flow and the delayed response from the PUPESDM regarding maintenance issues.

At this stage, there were some community groups who worried that the MHPP project would decrease irrigation water flows to their rice fields, but as they received explanations about how the plant operated, they understood and accepted setting up the MHPP in their area.

Adoption stage

During this trial period, communication was mainly between PUPESDM and the technicians. They used mobile phones as their main communication channel with content being mainly about technical aspects of the MHPP operation and its regular maintenance. The community felt that there was insufficient information on how to maintain the MHPP equipment and insufficient technical training on how to fix the machinery when there were broken parts. Community members also expected that they would receive information on how to manage the MHPP Organisation and on how to optimise the use of the MHPP in the future so that the community could benefit from its potential (Figure 5.4).

The hamlet leader chose five community representatives who ran home industries such as carpentry, egg farming and a mechanical workshop, to be pioneers to demonstrate the MHPP's benefits. Gradually, the number of households who connected to the MHPP increased as they understood its economic benefits: it could reduce their electricity costs and power basic home appliances. They affirmed it had increased their productive activities, not only during the day, but when it was dark. Street lighting in Kedungrong also made the community feel secure when they had evening activities and needed to travel around the hamlet at night. Snakes are a large issue, especially for children.

The incentive to form an MHPP Organisation came when the community realised that they needed to manage the operation. The MHPP Organisation consists of a head, vice head, bookkeeper and technicians. Their main duties are to monitor the use of the plant and ensure its maintenance, as well as managing the money collected as fees from their community. Every day, one member of the Organisation checks the flow of electricity generated and cleans up the rubbish in the irrigation canal to ensure no damage is caused to

Figure 5.4 Interview with a local businessman in Kedungrong Hamlet (photograph used with participants' permission)

the turbine. The community remarked that this maintenance requires certain skills and knowledge so not anyone could give practical support.

At the adoption stage, women's' groups expected to have direct information to and from PUPESDM and to be involved in discussions about the MHPP. Because MHPP issues are mostly discussed during the main hamlet meetings, women receive information largely second-hand from their husbands. However, women's groups also have regular meetings in which they expect to discuss the MHPP and via this route, they also expressed willingness to get involved in the MHPP Organisation.

Even though local Government representatives try to use direct communication channels such as text messaging, phone calls, or site visits, the community claimed that these channels are only used when they need to discuss technical problems. They also stated that when they contacted PUPESDM there were delays and they had to wait for answers, in fact they were uncertain that they would receive a response at all. Further, since there are no regular visits to the hamlet to monitor the MHPP operation, communities could not ask direct questions, neither did they have 'official' encouragement to maximise the use of MHPP. Other than the communication channels mentioned, the hamlet also wrote letters to PUPESDM. They found that such a formal approach enabled them to request assistance officially and ask for attention from local Government, but it did not speed up the communication process.

Transition stage

At the time of the research, there was an MHPP Organisation in Kedungrong already, run by volunteers. Their hard work was highly appreciated by community members, since not everybody was capable or willing to maintain the plant. Interestingly, we discovered that members of the MHPP Organisation committee were chosen based on their proximity to the plant rather than on their qualifications to undertake the work.

MHPP Organisations do not have a legal status or basic terms of reference and, as well as a need for training to run such an organisation, the hamlet claimed they need information and training that will enable them to be more technically proficient. They also indicated they would develop a better and legalised organisation after the MHPP was formally handed over to the community.

According to PUPESDM, the plant had already been handed over to the MHPP Organisation in Kedungrong. This was evidenced by a document signed by PUPESDM and local authorities at the Regency and Village level in 2015. This statement, however, was different from the information given to the researchers in the hamlet, including from members of the MHPP Organisation. They perceived that the MHPP was still the responsibility of PUPESDM and that they just needed to maintain the MHPP and use it for the benefit of communities. They were not aware that the MHPP had been handed over to them. Communication in this hamlet at this stage was, therefore, about maintaining the routine operational management of MHPP and they stated there had been no discussions on how to expand the utilisation of MHPP or preparations for them to take over ownership.

Sustainability stage

The perception that the MHPP was still owned by PUPESDM made the community reticent about developing further plans to enhance its use. They perceived that if PUPESDM planned to hand over the MHPP to them, PU-PESDM should make sure that the community had enough capability to manage it independently. Community leaders as well as the MHPP Organisation stated that they were not ready to manage the plant independently. Meanwhile, since formally the MHPP had been handed over to the community, PUPESDM could not provide a budget and technical support. What the findings suggest here is that there is an information gap that leads to an impasse in the development process. To be clear, the community wanted to own the MHPP and manage it independently, but only when they were capable of doing so. They also wanted their MHPP Organisation to have a legal status, which would then allow them to make choices about the use of the electricity, for example, whether to generate more to support community needs or to sell it to the national grid to gain more income for the hamlet.

The summary of the findings and recommendations from this case study are presented in Table 5.3.

Table 5.3 Findings and observations about Kedungrong Hamlet

Stage	Current condition	Gap	Recommendation
Pre-initiation	• The MHPP initiative emerged from the community. • Government approved and supported the initiative by conducting an FS, coordinating with related institutions and installing an MHPP with greater electricity generation capacity.	• Lack of clarity about the status and processes to support community-based MHPP initiatives.	• Clarify the status and process for community-initiated MHPP developments.

(Continued)

Table 5.3 (Continued)

Stage	Current condition	Gap	Recommendation
	• No strategic communication enacted by Government to engage with the community to ensure their participation.	• No discussion among community to exploit the usage of MHPP.	• Government needs a strategic communication approach to engage with communities to ensure their participation.
Adoption	• KKLPMD has become the main forum to discuss any issues related to MHPP. • PUPESDM communicates mainly with head of hamlet and MHPP technicians. • PUPESDM try to use direct communication channels, such as text message, phone calls, or site visits.	• Main forum is attended by community elite and household heads, most of whom are men. • Available communication channels are only used to discuss technical problems, no discussion on how to exploit the MHPP further.	• To ensure full support from all community groups, include their representatives in the MHPP Organisation. • Government should have interaction with the community using a wide variety of communication channels. • Government should widen discussions to cover more than just technical issues.
Transition	• PUPESDM only communicates with local authorities at the district and village level regarding the status of MHPP. • PUPESDM only refers to the formal requirement for handing over procedure, i.e. that there is a community based MHPP organisation in the hamlet.	• No information received by communities about the ownership status of MHPP, therefore they still fully rely on PUPESDM. • Hamlet communities perceive that the MHPP is PUPESDM's responsibility.	• Information about the ownership status of MHPP's should be clear and handover arrangements definitive: it affects the progress of community plans for MHPP and its fuller exploitation.

(*Continued*)

Table 5.3 (Continued)

Stage	Current condition	Gap	Recommendation
		• There is no training to enable the MHPP Organisation to manage MHPP effectively before and after the handing over process. • Communities and local officers worry that they are not ready to manage their MHPP, especially financial aspects.	
Sustainability	• Communities want to own their MHPP and manage it independently.	• Local Government did not conduct a preparation programme prior to the handover process.	• Government should instigate management training for MHPP Organisations before and after the handover.

Having presented the findings and initial recommendations from the three hamlet case studies themselves, the next chapter moves on to provide further analysis, discussing the findings and providing recommendations organised under the five stages of the project planning cycle given in Chapter 4.

6 Developing a new strategic participatory communication framework

A blueprint for empowerment

The results of the research outlined in Chapter 5 show that for development to be successful, the technical installation of MHPP cannot be separated from communication involving the communities concerned. Participatory communication is appropriate since this considers communities as collaborators in their own development rather than objects of development plans. This is a communication approach which relies on dialogue for sharing information, perceptions and opinions among all parties involved and empowers all, including those who are most vulnerable and marginalised.[1]

The strategic participatory communication framework

As described previously in Chapter 4, there are five stages to any Government development project: pre-initiation to sustainability. Given that we propose that communication is embedded throughout this process, this chapter discusses the findings under each stage and makes recommendations for changes. The resultant strategic communication framework to support MHPP development, Figure 6.1, is shown here rather later in this chapter because it underpins the proposals which is chapter explores.

Communication in the project life cycle of MHPP

The pre-initiation stage

MHPP development is initiated by conducting feasibility studies (FS) to choose geographic locations for potential development. There are two main activities at this stage, the FS itself and, if an area is chosen for development, socialisation of the FS results to the targeted communities.

As explained in Chapter 4, FSs are conducted by a consultant, appointed by Government at Province level (i.e. PUPESDM). Their job is to provide data for the Government on the viability of MHPPs in any locality, to choose the most suitable location for the plant as well as determining an appropriate

DOI: 10.4324/9781003507444-6

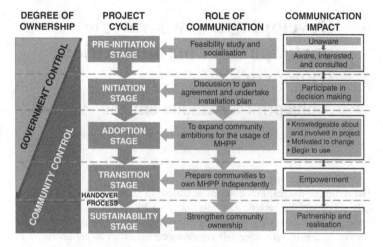

Figure 6.1 The Strategic Participatory Communication Framework linked to each stage of the project lifecycle[2]

design and budget. FSs do not engage directly with the affected communities; the actors are solely the Government and consultants. At this stage, communities are unaware that an MHPP is under consideration for their area. This is a significant flaw in the process given that local communities have intimate knowledge of their own locale and community and the evidence from the research shows a desire from them to be involved, even if the decision is eventually that the MHPP should not go ahead.

There is one important caveat to this. The research team agree with the order in which secondary data collection for the FS is undertaken. Technical data about the viability of a potential MHPP is collected first. If, from that technical data, it becomes very clear that an MHPP is not at all viable, communities should not be involved. This will avoid disappointment should their location not be selected for the project. However, if the secondary data indicates that there is some potential, it is at this point that communities can contribute their significant local knowledge to develop a fully informed FS, which can then be further supplemented with the additional information required in order for a licence to be granted.

Communication at the pre-initiation stage should be re-formulated as follows:

1   Include village communities at the pre-licence stage in the FS, at the point at which secondary data implies an MHPP is technically viable. Use information collected from them to inform the pre-licence FS.

2   Use this community data collection phase to build awareness about the potential MHPP and provide opportunities for all groups to gain information
about and input into the project.
3   When local Government makes a final decision about whether the project
should go ahead or not, one of two communication options should be taken:

    a   The community should be informed that the project will not go ahead
and be given reasons for this decision.
    b   The community should be informed that the MHPP will go ahead. At
this stage they can contribute more fully to the social and economic
elements of the licencing submission having had time to discuss their
aspirations (see initiation stage below).

4   The FS should not only focus on the technical specification of the MHPP
to fulfil the formal requirement to obtain the licence, but also aim to map
community groups, their assets and aspirations, assess initial community
support and identify who will be able to physically assist in the installation
and maintenance of the equipment.

Once the Government decides an MHPP will proceed, it must socialise the
decision and basic information on location, timescales, benefits etc., to the selected communities. Socialisation is conducted in the main community forum
involving community leaders and the heads of household (mainly male). To
date, the first time communities have been informed of an MHPP in their area
is during this socialisation process. This involvement, however, is passive
and positions communities as receivers, or objects, of decisions and information. Feedback or negotiation with them is not expected and communication
is largely tokenistic. Such a communication approach significantly limits the
opportunities for communities to actively embrace the project or contribute to
shaping its development.

The research team found that there was a deep desire to contribute, not only
in the main community group attended by key persons, but also in the wider
community such as in the women's, farmers and youth groups. Involving them
would draw on a deeper pool of knowledge and local wisdom and begin to
build whole community commitment – from the start of the project.

Socialisation in its current form, which is treated as a procedural part of
the FS, leads, the research has shown, to knowledge gaps about the MHPP
for both Government and the communities involved. This, in turn, creates
issues later and limits the efficient and effective implementation and potential of the project. Therefore, it is important to develop a communication
strategy that allows all parts of the community to access information, encourages questions and feedback and prompts direct and active participation
in the project.

Recommendations

1 At the socialisation stage, the emphasis should not be on the MHPP project's technical and process requirements only, but on securing the active buy-in of the community via knowledge sharing, encouraging participation in conversations and decisions, and generating excitement about the plant's potential.

2 Socialisation should also include a clear route map being provided by Government to the hamlet from initiation of the MHPP project to the point where they take over responsibility for it, with all the requisite steps being fully explained and access to information sources for each part of the journey being specified.

3 Communication should not only focus on key actors as individuals, but also on the whole community including households, community groups and networks.

The communication recommendations for the pre-initiation stage are illustrated in Figure 6.2.

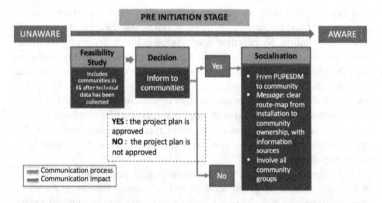

Figure 6.2 Communication recommendations for the pre-initiation stage[3]

The initiation stage

After the Government decides on where the MHPP is to be installed, the leader(s) of the hamlet(s) is/are informed in order to gain support from the community. The research found that even though there is no direct prior communication from local Government, communities are still willing to support the development and demonstrate this by volunteering labour and supporting workers who are hired by Government to build the MHPP. The community leader and technicians (chosen by the hamlet leader) who will help build and maintain the MHPP, become the key actors at this stage.

From this point, communities are aware that the Government will install an MHPP. What the study found, however, is that there is not sufficient information from the Government either about the installation plan, or about more general details such as benefits/impacts and reasonable expectations about the performance of the plant. Furthermore, the communication is restricted to local leaders and technicians.

Ideally, at this stage, communication would enable communities to be more knowledgeable and involved in the development, which can then motivate them to adopt the MHPP and be ready to exploit it. When they are not engaged from the beginning, the possibility for problems and failure increases. Good participative communication is not just about the Government informing communities so that it can achieve its own goals, but allows communities to co-create with Government what the goals for development should be. The researchers found that top-down communication results in limited participation, but when communities were encouraged to think through the potential of MHPP, horizons and ambitions were considerably expanded.

Recommendations

1 Installation intentions should be widely shared with communities to gain more support.
2 The MHPP installation plan should be developed and agreed by both PUPESDM and the community. Thus, the community becomes an actor in the installation development, not just a passive recipient. Figure 6.3 illustrates the recommended communication process.

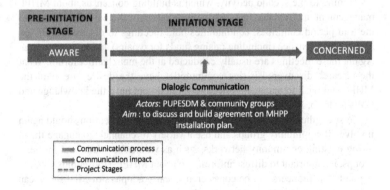

Figure 6.3 Communication recommendations for initiation stage

The adoption stage

The research found that communication at this stage can be divided into two main activities: 1) confirming and expanding details about MHPP benefits, and 2) building consensus among communities about MHPP management and maintenance.

During the equipment trial, communities are allowed to access electricity from the MHPP, such as to support street lighting and home industry activities. About five households, who own home industries, are chosen as pioneers and given access to electricity for their enterprises. Government regularly communicates with technicians to monitor the MHPP and to support their maintenance work.

More broadly, during the adoption stage, hamlets discuss the needs and hopes of the community in the main community forum, which is attended by community representatives. What is absent is the formal involvement of all community groups and the lack of information about the non-technical aspects of MHPP. Communities would like to know, from local Government, the full range of benefits (including social) and the most effective way to get the best from their MHPP.

Informally and individually, information about benefits and how to utilise the MHPP are shared among family and other community members. At the community level, technicians and pioneers share with their neighbours and, if a neighbouring *dusun* has adopted an MHPP earlier, they too will share information. Face-to-face communication and/or word of mouth is the main channel of communication.

The lack of informed input from local Government means that although hamlet members enthusiastically accept their MHPP, they are unsure of how to exploit it fully due to their limited knowledge and skills. Usage therefore remains restricted, for example, to street lighting and domestic appliances.

Turning to the second activity, which is building consensus about MHPP management and maintenance. As the installation of the MHPP finishes and the trial period continues, communities hold meetings to discuss MHPP usage and maintenance (including raising funds for repairs) and its exploitation. Again, these meetings are usually conducted at the main hamlet forum. What the research discovered is that communities have the desire to exploit the MHPP and wish to manage it effectively, but do not have the knowledge and skills to do so. No formal support is available.

To strengthen consensus and social support, communication should again involve all community groups and use a variety of channels to engage them. Using existing community networks, such as women's, youth, and farmer's groups, is important to diffuse information about MHPP. Households who are appointed as pioneers can be considered as early adopters of MHPP and can help promote new behaviours among their communities.

Communication is also more effective when using a) the local language commonly used in daily conversation and b) knowledge of how the community functions that is more culturally proximate. In essence, this involves recognising culture as a supportive factor rather than as a barrier to support positive change. It also means that Government should actively consider creating more opportunities to engage face-to-face with these communities.

Recommendations

At the adoption stage, communication should aim to move communities from awareness to knowledge and enquiry and further motivate them to try and exploit their MHPP. The recommendations for the communication strategy at this stage are:

1 to create knowledgeable and enquiring communities the Government should support by providing the variety and detail of information required and recommending appropriate actions, not just focus on technical operational matters;
2 the full range of community groups should be involved so that they in turn can provide mutual support and counsel to motivate the whole hamlet to adopt the MHPP fully;
3 a mixed communication approach is recommended, which combines both one-way and two-way dialogic communication. If communication aims to inform and persuade in order to raise awareness and increase knowledge, one-way communication can be used. However, if the aim is to explore, assess, analyse issues, solve problems and involve communities, then dialogic communication will be more appropriate. At this crucial adoption stage, dialogue should be the main approach taken to build support, surface issues and barriers, enhance collaboration, stimulate action and seek solutions to problems;
4 to encourage community participation and to build community consensus, deliberative techniques, specifically Appreciative Inquiry has proved effective in establishing consensus around a shared vision of the future, and to construct strategies and partnerships to achieve that vision[4];
5 the use of dialogue to promote participation, combined with the use of local language and knowledge are essential in encouraging community participation and consensus in the culture in which these MHPP developments take place;
6 technicians and champions have a crucial role to play in motivating communities to exploit the MHPP;
7 during the trial period, as well as regular consultation with local Government, and ongoing monitoring and evaluation of MHPP performance and

usage, an initial evaluation of community readiness to manage the MHPP independently should be conducted.

8   the results of regular monitoring and evaluation provide essential management information and can be used by local Government not only for understanding local and technical issues, but for identifying other systemic problems, as a basis for ongoing discussions with communities and to refine and smooth the national renewable energy project as a whole.

The recommendations for the adoption stage are illustrated as shown in Figure 6.4

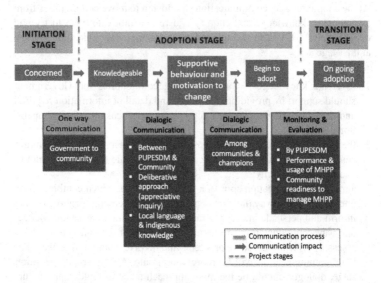

Figure 6.4 Communication recommendations for adoption stage

The transition stage

At this stage, the assumption is that the community has adopted and started to ramp up the use of the MHPP. The communication, accordingly, aims to prepare communities to take ownership of the plant and they need to form an MHPP Organisation.

As observed in case study three, there is no rejection by the community of the MHPP, quite the reverse; they claim they have gained economic as well as social benefits. However, this case also shows, there was lack of community knowledge and skills to fully exploit the MHPP. Furthermore, there is no formal programme for preparing communities to independently manage it, although the community expressed a desire to learn these skills. Training aimed at empowering communities to operationalise their development ambitions is required, tailored to meet the choices they have made. If the Government is unable to provide such a training offer, third parties could be employed to support this process.

Recommendations

To prepare communities to own and manage their MHPP independently, communication at this stage should be focused on assuring them of their ability to sustain their plant and their ambitions for developing their lives economically and socially. The recommendations for the communication strategy at this stage are:

1 a clear route-map and guidance to be provided by Government and discussed with the community on the technical preparedness required to take over operation of the plant, along with requisite training on managing MHPP operations and organisations;
2 negotiation and discussion on when the plant is ready to be handed over to communities. The date of hand-over is currently dictated by time alone (three years from the creation of the MHPP Organisation);
3 ongoing discussions with local Government or third parties using a deliberative approach to help communities to identify current and future social and economic developments such as ecotourism or home industries;
4 identification of training needs to build community capability and capacity (at all levels, from leader down) to fully exploit opportunities;
5 access provided to that training. Training to be used not only to build long-term community capacity, but a means to achieve positive social change.

The recommendations above are illustrated as shown in Figure 6.5

The sustainability stage

By the end of year three after the MHPP Organisation is established and operates independently, Government hands over full responsibility to the community. The study found that the handover process consists of paperwork procedures only and there are no other preparations prior to that. Information about ownership status and its consequences are not communicated clearly to communities and as a result, they are confused about who owns the MHPP, the point at which they take over ownership and what their respective responsibilities are. They feel unready to manage the operation of the plant by themselves, especially the financial aspects and unsure how they can exploit the MHPP further and into the future.

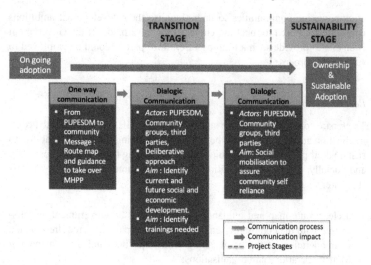

Figure 6.5 Communication recommendations for transition stage

The research also found that communities need ongoing support because their ambitions and aspirations continue to develop. They require ongoing capability development both to support the full exploitation of the plant (for example, if they want to sell electricity to the national grid) and to realise their economic and social aspirations.

Recommendations

The assumption in these recommendations is that the communities will have agreed the hand over, that economic opportunities have been explored and training has been undertaken. Further, it is assumed that consultancy support (see below) to the community has begun during the trial phase. The focus here is to cement community ownership and sustain activity in exploiting the potential of MHPP.

Recommendations to achieve this ideal are as follows:

1   improve community capability on an ongoing basis by involving third parties such as Government agencies, for example, tourism, trade and cooperative agencies, and non-Government institutions, such as universities or NGOs to support through coaching, mentoring, training and consultancy;
2   make available ongoing technical and managerial consultancy to support communities;

3 assist in partnership development with, for example, entrepreneurs and tourism organisations etc.;

4 involve communities through their forums and groups to develop ongoing sustainable programs for their MHPP and include them in the village/ *dusun* development plan to secure funding: short (annual programme), medium (5 years plan), and long (25 years plan), to ensure on-going development;

5 maintain communication and relationships with Government to provide updates on the status of the MHPP (so Government has first-hand management information and intelligence to inform policy) and on Government policy (to the communities) so that they can be fully informed.

These recommendations are provided in diagrammatic form in Figure 6.6.

Figure 6.6 Communication recommendations for the sustainability stage

A strategic participatory communication blueprint

Having identified clear communication needs and recommendations from the research, it is now possible to put together a strategic participatory communication blueprint, see Table 6.1, which can be implemented alongside the technical project cycle. It can also be used as part of the process to install any type of renewable energy project in rural communities, or for broader-based infrastructure projects.

Table 6.1 Strategic participatory communication blueprint

Project cycle	Project goals	Communication process	Project outputs	Communication outcomes	Communication components
PRE-INITIATION STAGE	To obtain an assessment of the potential for an MHPP To decide where it should be located	Feasibility study (FS)	Targeted location for MHPP	**Unaware** → **Aware**	• *Aim:* fulfil the technical requirements for the MHPP; map community groups, their assets and aspirations; assess initial community support; identify who will be able to assist physically in the installation and maintenance of the MHPP. • *Actors:* Government, FS consultant, village/hamlet communities • *Content:* if project is physically viable, information *from* Government to communities about proposed MHPP and their decision, whether the project will go ahead or not. Information *to* Government from communities; information for FS; community assets, level of support and aspirations • *Channels:* community leader and hamlet forums of all types, mainly face-to-face, but other channels e.g. mobile phone, some visual and written material if required. *Informing and consultative* approach

(Continued)

Table 6.1 (Continued)

Project cycle	Project goals	Communication process	Project outputs	Communication outcomes	Communication components
	To socialise the FSs results	Socialisation	To complete 'licence to operate' requirements	**Aware**	• *Aim*: To secure active buy-in of community via knowledge sharing, participation in decisions and raising excitement about *potential of MHPP.* • *Actors*: Government, MHPP consultant, households, community groups and networks • Content: *From Government*: technical requirements for the MHPP installation; route-map on path to ownership of MHPP by hamlet. *To Government* local knowledge to inform decision-making and provide intelligence for licence application. • *Channels/method*: community forums, written and visual materials, open communication channels for further information (e.g. telephone, SMS, village visits – needs to be structured to manage process well). Dialogic in character approach i.e. *involving* approach

(Continued)

Table 6.1 (Continued)

Project cycle	Project goals	Communication process	Project outputs	Communication outcomes	Communication components
INITIATION STAGE	To install the MHPP	• Community-based meetings to agree involvement in MHPP installation process • MHPP technical training from the Government for 3 to 5 volunteers	• Installation plan • Three to five MHPP-trained technicians	(arrow) **Concerned** **Motivation to adopt**	• *Aim*: to gain agreement on the installation plan • *Actors*: Government, community groups, technicians, MHPP construction contractor • *Content*: about the installation plan which results in agreement on goals by Government and communities • *Channels/method*: a range of methods under the deliberative umbrella, e.g. using Appreciative Inquiry in community forums, interviews with technicians, FGDs with women's and youth groups. *Involving* approach.
ADOPTION STAGE	To trial the MHPP	• Dialogic communication involving a range of actors	• Effective trialling of equipment by hamlet	(arrow) **Knowledgeable**	• *Aim*: to try out the MHPP and to motivate communities to adopt MHPP. • *Actors*: Government, technicians, potential champions, community groups

(Continued)

Table 6.1 (Continued)

Project cycle	Project goals	Communication process	Project outputs	Communication outcomes	Communication components
		• Hamlet trials MHPP assisted by pro-active support by Government: five households appointed as champions	• Consensus on MHPP management • Consideration of MHPP Organisation	**Supportive behaviour and motivation to adopt** →	• *Content*: the day-to-day usage and maintenance of MHPP; benefits and barriers to adopting the MHPP; appropriate actions to overcome the barriers • *Channels/method*: deliberative approach, using a range of methods i.e. Appreciative Inquiry in community forum
		• Regular consultation with local Government • On-going monitoring and evaluation by Government	• Report on MHPP performance and usage, and evaluation. • Initial evaluation of community readiness to manage the MHPP	**Begin to adopt** →	• *Aim*: to monitor and evaluate MHPP performance and usage, as well as community readiness to manage the MHPP • *Actors*: Government, technicians, community • *Content*: the issues and solutions to community management of MHPP usage and maintenance, community readiness to adopt the MHPP • *Channels/method*: regular discussions in community groups; monthly reports from the technicians to Government; regular visits from the Government to the community. Approach – *Informing and Involving*

(Continued)

Table 6.1 (Continued)

Project cycle	Project goals	Communication process	Project outputs	Communication outcomes	Communication components
Transition Stage	To prepare the MHPP management and operational infrastructure prior to MHPP handover	• One-way communication from Government to the community on regulatory process • Dialogic communication using deliberative approach to ensure understanding and commitment • Training for communities and MHPP Organisation	• Setting up of MHPP Organisation • Preparation of hamlet community to take over ownership of MHPP • Training	**Full adoption**	• *Aims*: to identify current and future social and economic development: build community capability and capacity to take over and exploit their MHPP • *Actors*: Government, community groups, MHPP Organisation, third parties • *Content*: clear route map on handover process; guidance to hamlet on MHPP Organisation set-up; identification of economic and social development using MHPP; training needs analysis; training provision; consultative advice • *Channel/ method*: deliberative and participatory i.e. appreciative inquiry in community forums and groups, FGDs; face-to-face interactions with Government; training. Approach – Informing and *Partnering*

(Continued)

Table 6.1 (Continued)

Project cycle	Project goals	Communication process	Project outputs	Communication outcomes	Communication components
Sustainability Stage	To assure the community has self-determination to exploit the MHPP.	• Ongoing consultancy • Partnership with a range of actors • Coaching, mentoring training to build capability	• Improved community capability • Long-term sustainable program for MHPP use and development in hamlet	**Ownership & Sustainable Exploitation** ➡	• *Aims*: improve community capability to exploit MHPP, enable community to develop sustainable programs for MHPP, strengthen community ownership of MHPP • *Actors*: MHPP organisation, community groups, third parties, Government • *Content*: potential partnership programmes, training etc. needs, training etc. provision • *Channel/ method*: deliberative e.g. appreciative inquiry, using community forums and groups; consultation; training. *Partnering* approach.
		• Maintain communication and relationship with the Government	• Update information about MHPP and Government policy and lessons are learned		• *Aim*: to ensure Government policy is informed by field-based intelligence and community informed of new Government policies. • *Actors*: MHPP Organisation, Government • *Content*: updated information about MHPP, economic and social development • *Channel/ method*: direct communication (e.g. face-to-face communication), mediated communication (e.g. by phone, emails). A regular feedback mechanism should be established. *Partnering* approach

This blueprint provides guidelines on how participatory communication should be conducted throughout the MHPP project lifecycle. The recommendations are laid out systematically following the five stages of the MHPP project lifecycle. It describes the goals associated with each stage of the lifecycle and the communication processes involved to achieve project outputs. Also included are the communication outcomes that will be achieved and the components of communication plans for each element of the project lifecycle.

Using this blueprint, the projected outcomes of strategic participatory communication are:

1 increased feelings of ownership of their MHPP among communities and their commitment to its future exploitation;
2 improved community competency and capacity to engage with and exploit their MHPP;
3 sustainable behaviour changes leading to full adoption and exploitation of MHPP post-installation and when communities take over ownership;
4 community empowerment;
5 achievement of Government objectives in rural sustainable energy, economic development and poverty reduction.

The transformational effects in the communication approach from where it currently stands to where it ideally should be, can be readily explained. In simplified form, currently rural communities at the hamlet level are *informed* that they will receive an MHPP at the point at which the FS has been completed. They are *told* what will happen and what the potential benefits can be. Thereafter the communication largely concerns maintaining and monitoring the MHPP equipment so that the community can own it three years after an MHPP Organisation has been formed. Technicians and hamlet elite groups are involved in this process, but in an unsystematic way and not about all the topics and issues that concern and interest them. Technical considerations dominate. Furthermore, many other groups within communities are not fully informed or involved.

The purpose of this new approach to communication is to involve and galvanise the whole community so that they all take ownership of their MHPP and through the process become empowered to take a level of self-determination for their future. *Partnership* between Government and local communities is what should characterise this process. Both sides of the partnership have much to contribute and to learn from the other. Through this new way of working, Government is more likely to achieve its national renewable energy aspirations and rural communities can develop, both economically and socially.

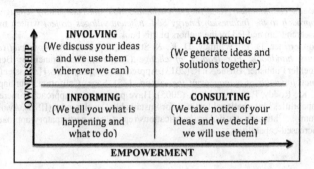

Figure 6.7 Community ownership and empowerment increased through participatory communication

Figure 6.7 indicates how ownership and empowerment go hand in hand with a communication approach that progressively involves communities. The proposal is that communication moves from being based on *informing,* with Government doing this 'top down', through to *consulting* (as the community itself gains capability to contribute) to *involving* and eventually *partnering* as they are equipped to do so. In fact, this can be done relatively rapidly with the use of skilled facilitators and the right participatory communication techniques. There is no lack of desire to be involved in communities as the researchers have discovered and having been given the opportunity and the training to do this competently, no lack of ideas to manage, operate and exploit their renewable energy resource.

As argued in Chapter 1, the research team have approached this project not only to develop a communication blueprint for MHPP development in Indonesia, but to provide a transferable strategic tool that can be contextualised and operationalised for any Government, private sector or NGO to utilise. The next chapter demonstrates how the blueprint can be adopted by private-sector organisations.

Notes

1 Tufte, T., & Mefalopulos, P. (2009). *Participatory communication: A practical guide*. World Bank: Washington, D.C.
2 Figure taken from Yudarwati, G.A. & Gregory, A. (2022). Improving government communication and empowering rural communities: Combining public relations and development communication approaches. *Public Relations Review*, 48 (3), article 102200.
3 Permission to reproduce Figures 6.1 to 6.7 has been obtained from British Council Newton Fund Institutional Links Programme Grant Application ID 217488952. These Figures were included in the Report *Transitions towards renewable energy*

based: communities: A strategic communication and community engagement approach to the Indonesian Energy Self-sufficient villages project written by the research team and led by the authors of this book.

4 Cooperrider, D. L., Whitney, D. K. & Stavros, J. M. (2008). *Appreciative Inquiry handbook: For leaders of change* (2nd ed.), San Francisco: Berrett-Koehler Publisher; Bushe, G. R. (2013). Appreciative inquiry. In: E. H. Kessler (ed.), *Encyclopaedia of management theory* (pp. 1–5). Sage: California; Duraiappah, A. K., Roddy, P. & Parry, J.-E. (2005). Have participatory approaches increased capabilities? International Institute for Sustainable Development (IISD). Available from: https://www.iisd.org/publications/report/have-participatory-approaches-increased-capabilities

7 Applying the participatory model in other contexts

The research described in previous chapters was completed in the context of Government engagement with local communities, but the lessons are applicable to other large organisations who want to build meaningful engagement programmes. This chapter illustrates how the proposed approaches can work for other types of organisations, in different for-profit sectors. It provides lessons learned from multinational companies operating in Indonesia who seek to engage communities in the implementation of their corporate social responsibility (CSR) initiatives. CSR practice for such large companies often includes development initiatives in countries at a similar stage of economic and social progress as Indonesia.

The context of multinational companies

Most multinational companies, by definition, are organisations operating across a range of territories, drawing on local populations and resources for their own progress. They are major forces in worldwide economic development and their contribution to the economic growth of developing countries is unquestioned. As emerging markets, developing countries represent both opportunities and risks for multinationals. With billions of customers, developing countries offer a huge market opportunity, but doing business in them can pose challenges. Weak public governance and transparency, endemic nepotism, bribery and corruption, low health, safety and environmental standards, as well as high levels of poverty and inequality all bring their problems. At the same time, multinational companies have been criticised for pursuing profits in developing countries while exploiting workforces and the environment. In response to such concerns, they have increasingly taken action to engage closely with local stakeholders while also demonstrating their responsibility through CSR initiatives.

CSR practices by multinational companies have raised important issues about what can be considered universal and what needs adaptation to local contexts. They have been criticised for enforcing a Western view of CSR throughout their global operations. This is because they enact policies that do

DOI: 10.4324/9781003507444-7

not represent global standards based on 'universal' concerns as they claim, but which reflect Western ideals which are acceptable to shareholders, many of whom are Western. Nevertheless, multinational companies need to consider the different societal and governmental pressures exerted in home versus host countries and to develop strategies to address cross-cultural diversity and conflicts in order to gain local acceptance.

It has been argued that multinational companies' commitment to CSR has resulted from public pressures from host and home countries as well as international stakeholders. Societal concerns directed to companies by stakeholders can be various and often conflicting. In-country Governments emphasise the importance of public–private partnership to develop the community. Consumer groups are concerned with product quality, provenance and production processes. Environmentalists focus on the environmental impact of corporations. Each defines CSR in line with their perception of specific situations and challenges.

Moreover, there is an ongoing debate on whether there should be a global CSR approach or a decentralised, local one. For multinational companies who need to operate in a host country, the implementation of CSR policies is complex because of the many multicultural contexts in which they operate. They need to work with people and companies from a range of countries or areas with very different values and expectations. In implementing CSR strategies the ideal position is that they recognise and respect local and cultural differences, while at the same time, maintaining global standards and policies. Implementing this ideal is difficult and requires engagement in open dialogue and partnerships with Governments of host countries, NGOs and, in particular, local communities with all their differing, and sometimes competing, interests and cultures.

Institutional factors that shape company's stakeholder engagement

CSR is shaped by three major institutional factors: regulatory, professional and public.[1] Regulatory pressures come from governing stakeholders, including Governments and regulatory agencies. Professional pressures include those from professional associations in the industry sector who press for specific CSR practices. Lastly, CSR is also shaped by pressures from societal stakeholders such as customers and local communities, who demand multinationals to comply with their socially constructed expectations. The combination of these three sources of pressure leads to two major factors that shape CSR policy as identified by multinational companies: (1) different regulatory and governance standards between home and host countries and (2) community expectations and culture.

Factor 1: Different regulatory and governance standards between home and host countries

Different regulatory and governance standards, as shown in Table 7.1, have generated risks for companies. Most multinational companies are headquartered in developed countries and have operations in developing countries, where the regulatory environment in the home country is often more rigorous than in the host country. These discrepancies in regulatory environments provide a challenge, but also an opportunity for operations overseas. In developed countries, which have a very strong regulatory environment, not only are companies themselves subject to strict processes, but so is the way they deal with communities, especially those who are indigenous or

Table 7.1 Worldwide governance indicators (in 2022)[2]

Indicator	Country	Percentile rank (0–100)
Voice and accountability	Australia	93.24
	France	85.99
	Indonesia	52.66
	United Kingdom	89.37
	United States	72.95
Political stability and absence of violence/terrorism	Australia	81.6
	France	56.13
	Indonesia	29.25
	United Kingdom	62.26
	United States	45.28
Government effectiveness	Australia	92.92
	France	83.02
	Indonesia	66.04
	United Kingdom	85.85
	United States	86.79
Regulatory quality	Australia	99.53
	France	85.38
	Indonesia	59.43
	United Kingdom	93.40
	United States	91.04
Rule of law	Australia	91.04
	France	85.38
	Indonesia	45.28
	United Kingdom	89.15
	United States	88.68
Control of corruption	Australia	95.28
	France	85.38
	Indonesia	37.74
	United Kingdom	92.92
	United States	82.55

marginalised. A strongly regulated environment provides clear structures on how to conduct business, but has also been perceived as burdensome and pressurising. There is less pressure in host countries, but corruption issues within local Government and the host countries' inability to comply with global standards due to lack of resources or capability, have become a liability for multinational companies.

With these complexities, multinational companies experience three challenges in mediating their businesses in host countries: (1) how to manage their business while also complying with home country and global standards, (2) how to manage relationships with local Government who have different regulatory and governance standards and (3) how to maintain relationships with corporate head office, who have their own reporting requirements internally for the Board and who expect to see good performance from all parts of the group. In addition, corporate (Head Office) management asserts that their stakeholders are global public and organisations. They are acutely aware of global pressures for maintaining good governance in business practices and investment in sustainable development. Therefore, to gain global recognition and acceptance, they choose to enact global standards of CSR that are not negotiable.

If there is an expectation for compliance to local regulatory requirements, it is often limited to those regulated and legal areas drafted under foreign direct investment agreements signed by companies. A way forwards on CSR, which is non-regulatory, is to commit to improve capability and capacity in the management team in the host countries in order to encourage better governance.

Factor 2: Community's expectations and culture

Multinational companies often operate in countries with different cultures. As has been noted throughout this book, communities in host countries are complex with strong cultural bonds and traditional structures. It is more difficult for multinationals to 'manage' people with different cultural backgrounds and demands, than to manage their technical operations, which tend to be comparable whenever they operate. As an example, multinational mining companies often encounter three main issues that can lead to conflicts between the company and its host community: land, local employment and local contractors who quite reasonably want to gain work from the company, but whose expertise/skills/working standards are not in line with the company's standards.[3]

Land acquisition is potentially the greatest source of conflict because of ongoing disputes between mining law and *adat* or cultural law with regard to its ownership. There is also a community belief that land is part of cultural heritage, which is not commercially compensable. The emphasis on group goals over personal goals and their strong attachment to and followership of their leaders means companies have to approach ethnic group leaders as well as *adat* leaders to obtain acceptance and approval from them. If these community leaders agree to company proposals conflicts can be prevented, but if they fail to reach agreement, it is unlikely community members will give up their land. In addition, the concept of 'in-group' and 'out-group' means that people, including companies in the 'out-group being regarded with caution. Collectivism, strong spiritual beliefs and cultural traditions, and the use of ethnic language, to name a few, are other cultural values that need to be considered in host countries.

A number of multinational companies operating in Bali, Indonesia, such as Danone Indonesia, Coca-Cola Europacific Partners, and international hotel chains such as Marriott or Four Seasons, are well aware of these considerations. For example, they are conscious that certain employees need to follow ritual ceremonies, some lasting a day, but some requiring more than a week. They therefore adjust holiday and leave policies to accommodate this and during the fasting month of Ramadan, adjust working hours for Moslem communities.

Not all local values create barriers for companies. The togetherness of collectivist communities is a social capital that can be used to encourage them participate in CSR initiatives for the common good. *Ngayah* for Balinese or *gotong rotong* for Javanese, a willingness to participate and work voluntarily, can be assets for companies. The *Tri Hita Karana*, which is a Balinese spiritual philosophy of maintaining harmony with God, others and the environment, embodies values in line with the sustainability initiatives aimed at mitigating negative environmental impacts. Thus, what is suggested here is that multinational companies must navigate unavoidable different cultural values as they seek to secure their business and live harmoniously with local communities.

Community and communication engagement

As discussed in Chapter 1, our book is not about arguing which approach to development is right or wrong, but about how organisations show willingness to understand and incorporate different perspectives in conducting their business. So, how can this be achieved in practical terms?

To illustrate this, we researched six multinational companies who operate in Indonesia, categorised as being in the primary, secondary and tertiary sectors, as shown in Table 7.2. This categorisation is based on the contribution of the industry to the country, as well as the impacts of the industry to the environment and social livelihood.

Table 7.2 The six multi-national companies by industry sector

Category	Types of industry	Numbers of company
Primary sector	Mining	2
	Oil and gas	1
Secondary sector	Steel	1
	Food and beverages	1
Tertiary sector	Banking	1
TOTAL		6

Assigning field officers who have the same cultural background as the community and/or who are aware of cultural differences

To engage with communities, multinational companies in the primary sector, who heavily depend on local resources and significantly change the livelihood of communities, have established a dedicated community relations and development unit which resides in the affected communities. The companies hire community members who have the same cultural background, or have a good understanding of cultural differences, to be their field officers. The responsibilities of these field officers, who are mostly those with a respected social status, such as teachers or those with a high caste, include engaging with communities and exploring communities needs and attitudes. They are also responsible for articulating the needs of minority and more marginalised parts of their communities, so that potential points of conflict can be understood and addressed. By having the same cultural background and language as the community, it is more likely that field officers are accepted by them. Such an arrangement recognises the concepts of 'in-group' and 'out-group' and collective community.

Local communities are aware that these field officers work for companies, but they trust that field officers will not betray them since that goes against their shared cultural values. Besides acting as cultural interpreters between companies and communities field officers serve as a model for communities. If a company initiates a sustainability initiative, for instance, it is likely that whole communities will trust and follow the suggested behaviours as modelled by company field officers.

In the case of companies in secondary and tertiary industries, they do not need to establish a dedicated community relations and development unit within communities. Rather, they acknowledge the importance of having representatives who can liaise with communities on initiating and implementing specific CSR programmes. Their activities tend to be project-based rather than ongoing. For instance, to run local waste management or organic farming programmes, the companies will recruit and train a community representative.

In the Government project previously described in this book, local leaders at village and hamlet levels become the gatekeepers of community engagement. These leaders are elected by communities and are presented by district leaders to the regency/city for approval. Thus, because of their formal position and link to Government, they have significant positions as middle persons between Government and local communities. However, in the case of non-Government organisations, such as multinational companies, these local leaders often only provide permission to the companies to enter communities. That is why companies also need to identify and engage with other local leaders, such as religious leaders or elderly people, and assign field officers or project representatives, who will directly and actively engage and immerse themselves within communities.

Enacting sensing process and social mapping

From the very early stage of their operations, multinational companies allocate resources and put effort to understand their environment and community dynamics by undertaking what they call *sensing* and *social mapping*. Referring to the previous chapters, this is a process comparable to that which is recommended in the feasibility studies. The difference is that in the Government project, the feasibility study was assisted by an external consulting team. For multinational companies it is assisted by field officers who immerse themselves in communities by, for example, going to local restaurants and socialising with local people to get a sense of what is important for them. Through this process, companies identify community structure, social dynamics, understand their demands, tensions and anxieties, as well as what makes them happy or afraid. They can also identify key community actors who may have the power to attribute legitimacy to them and their work.

Encouraging community participation

These multinational companies have changed their approach in implementing CSR programmes, from merely charity or top-down company gifts to more participatory programmes that involve communities. Their field officers or project representatives not only share information about CSR programmes, but also absorb community needs and opinions by conducting focus group discussions, holding meetings with community leaders and other community representatives, or by attending the *Musrenbang*. This aim is to encourage community participation, build commitment and the ambition is to include CSR programmes in hamlet and village development plans in order to ensure their sustainability.

We have mapped the process in Figure 7.1, which can be seen to have parallels with Figure 6.1 in Chapter 6.

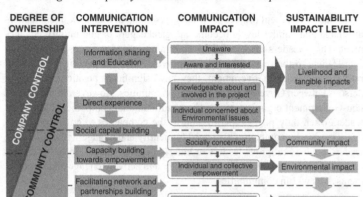

Figure 7.1 Community engagement for company CSR programmes in Indonesia

The process starts by showing the livelihood and tangible impacts of CSR programmes to communities. Information-sharing sessions and education for communities can transform them from unaware to becoming aware and interested to participate in the programme. Providing information only through one-way communication is not regarded as adequate to gain support. Communities will act only when they understand the practical value of the information they have received.

Accordingly, the process includes disclosing direct experiences that allow communities to see what to do and how to participate, as well as how easy or difficult it is to be involved. For example, to encourage the adoption of organic farming, the economic factor, i.e. a competitive price of organic rice in the market, is a potential magnet to attract community interest. The adoption of organic farming by a pioneer, who is chosen from the community, provides a practical example that leads to acceptance of the programme.

Similarly, a community-based waste bank, which collects and sorts solid waste is part of a waste management programme which combines economic and environment benefits. This programme is based in Bali, Indonesia, whose communities hold the *Tri hita karana* philosophy: these, economic and spiritual values have become entry points to encourage community participation. To extend the programme's benefit and build ownership, sharing experiences in regular meetings or conducting collection activities are some interventions to build social capital, which is significant to achieving collective community impact. Furthermore, community members, individually and/or collectively, can make their own decisions about whether to adopt the program, thereby giving them a level of agency in decisions about their own lives.

Engagement activities also include capacity-building programmes that enable them to gain confidence, knowledge and skills to deal with social change. For example, in the areas where mining has become significant, operations radically change community livelihoods. Prior to the presence of this industry, communities relied on farming but needed to change their income sources to survive as large areas of farmland were given over to mining. Through CSR programmes, companies provide communities with capacity-building programmes to acquire new skills such as running restaurants, food production or eco-tourism.

In the secondary industry sector, the food and beverages company supports waste management by providing 3R (reuse, reduce and recycle) training for communities. Recycling instruction includes skills training in creating handicrafts from plastic waste. In the tertiary industry, the bank not only provides below-market interest rate loans to community groups to set up small businesses, but also offers training in financial management.

To ensure sustainability, the engagement process outlined here requires participation from third parties, such as distributors, other business partners and universities to enhance community knowledge and networks in order to expand opportunities. Similar to the transfer of power and ownership from Government to communities, this engagement process suggests the same from companies to communities. Figure 7.1 indicates the whole process has similarities with the model discussed in previous chapters, although it is not as developed.

In encouraging community participation, four factors have been highlighted through the research with companies. First, it is important to initiate the engagement through key actors within the community, i.e. field officers, company representatives, or community leaders because this addresses essential elements in the collectivism culture. These key actors can be the role models, from whom communities learn through observation, imitation, and modelling. Second, it is important to acknowledge local values and knowledge, as well as to envision empowerment through the collective action of all parties involved. Third, companies recognise the lack of community skills and knowledge when significant change is proposed. Accordingly, capacity building, often involving third parties, is a major part of their development work. Finally, networking and partnership facilitation are required as companies gradually transfer programme ownership to the communities. All these elements are present in the desired Government engagement approach too.

Having explored a new model for Government/community engagement for infrastructure development and having seen how parts of the proposed model are mirrored in current multinational corporate CSR practices, it is timely to draw together some reflections and conclusions. This is done in the following chapter.

Notes

1   Yudarwati, G.A., Sison, M.D., Putranto, I.A. & Wiratsari, P. (2023). Enacting institutional drivers towards strategic corporate social responsibility: The sensemaking process in multinational companies. *Corporate Social Responsibility and Environmental Management*, 30(4), 1782–1793.
2   Kaufmann, D. and Kraay, A. (2023). Worldwide governance indicators, 2023 Update. Available at www.govindicators.org (Accessed 10.08.2024)
3   Yudarwati, G.A. & Tjiptono, F. (2017). An enactment theory perspective of corporate social responsibility and public relations. *Marketing Intelligence & Planning*, 35(5), 626–640.

8 Final thoughts

This book describes the research undertaken in a two-year project funded by a British Council Institutional Links Newton Fund grant and the Strategic Participatory Communication Framework that has been built on the findings. The aim of the original project was to support rural communities in Indonesia in their transition from intermittent carbon-generated electricity drawn from the National Grid to local renewable energy sources.

We found that while the physical installation of renewable energy infrastructure has been well supported by Government, the full potential of these projects is not always being realised. A reason for this is that rural communities are not involved in ways that they regard as meaning-ful: these energy projects are 'imposed' on them. A consequence is that indigenous knowledge and aspirations are not sought and used and there-fore there is a lack of a sense of local ownership of these projects. This in turn leads to a lukewarm enthusiasm and while the obvious and im-mediate benefits of locally based renewable energy are grasped, such as street lighting and powering domestic appliances, the more imaginative and transformative uses, such as for example, small industry develop-ment, are left untapped.

The research shows that there is no lack of willingness on behalf of rural communities to be more involved in sustainable energy pro-jects, but there are a number of cultural, social and process gaps, which need to be bridged. One of the practical measures that can be taken is to embed strategic communication as an integral part of the infrastructure project life cycle. The Strategic Participatory Communication Frame-work provides the approach for this with the Strategic Participatory Communication Blueprint outlining the practical steps that can be taken in MHPP installation.

Chapter 7 has shown that some of the main principles of the Strategic Participatory Communication Framework are being applied in alterna-tive settings, thereby evidencing that the Framework is robust and can be transferable.

DOI: 10.4324/9781003507444-8

Conclusions

We have drawn several conclusions from this work. First, rural communities have huge economic and social potential. Strategic communication can help them articulate, understand the worth of and realise that potential. Second, while it may take some additional time and resources to embed strategic participatory communication in the infrastructure development life cycle, this is more than offset by the benefits that accrue to both communities and Governments:

- Rural communities benefit through the additional economic activity that will be stimulated, which makes them more economically sustainable. In addition, it builds social bonds in the community as they determine their future together.
- The ambitions of Government sustainable energy policy can be more fully enacted when physical infrastructure development is supported by strategic communication.
- The co-operative capital that is built between Government and rural communities is worth the investment.

Third, additional benefits such as rural self-determination, empowerment and poverty reduction are all realisable objectives if the aspirations and capacity of rural communities are raised through strategic communication.

Fourth, Government can open an invaluable channel of management information by engaging in dialogic communication with rural communities. This will help to inform current policy implementation and assist future policy development by harnessing field-based intelligence that is unmediated. This understanding identified a requirement to develop informal and formal feedback mechanisms with rural communities and curate that information so that local and national Government can draw on the significant intelligence that resides in them to inform current policy implementation and future policy development.

Fifth, the principles of strategic participatory communication identified in this research and which apply to MHPP projects can be generalised for other sustainable energy sources in Indonesia such as solar and biomass. Furthermore, these principles can be applied to community-based infrastructure projects more broadly, not only in Indonesia, but in other similar cultures in the ASEAN region. Indeed, while there is no evidence yet, there is reason to believe that these principles are widely applicable in the emerging and developing nations of the Global South. It is part of the human condition, once basic needs have been met, to strive to satisfy higher needs such as a sense of belonging, esteem and self-actualisation.[1] In other words, once the basic level of subsistence farming has been achieved and communities can feed and shelter themselves, they will seek ways to advance themselves in whatever terms they would describe that. Rather than having others dictate how, what and when that advancement should look like, they will receive greater satisfaction and give greater commitment to a future which they have had a voice in shaping. More than that, their local cultural and contextual knowledge is crucial in advancing development plans that are realistic and realisable.

Learning and insights

We have also taken many learnings and insights from this project.

Giving people a voice and respecting their knowledge is empowering for them. We have been surprised by the ambition of these communities. This partly speaks to our own patronising views which have build-up over years of assuming that those who do manual, subsistence labour are somehow incapable of ambition. The fact that many of the young people of these communities are leaving to seek 'a better life' gives the lie to that. More than that, it was clear that given the opportunity to speak and when we really listened, there was no shortage of ideas and no shortage of vision. All we did was to give them the tools, through participatory communication, to be able to explore their possible futures and help them believe that they were possible. They raised their own ambitions and were excited by them.

We realised that it was not only Government that provided the resources for development projects, although many such projects are currently framed as such. NGOs and other rural development partners are sources of funding and expertise to be drawn on. They have their own agendas, but they are also open to approaches from communities who can articulate their plans and demonstrate their commitment. Breaking the long-learned and comfortable cycle of dependency on Government will be a way for communities to enact their empowerment. For example, many private sector organisations have corporate social responsibility programmes that will offer business development expertise, volunteer help and funds. Tourism organisations are keen to capitalise on the growing interest in eco and sustainable tourism. The realisation that they can negotiate their future with such organisations is empowering and enriching for these communities.

Finally, we understood what a crucial role education and training has in empowering communities. Initially, technicians needed training (provided by Government) to operate and maintain the MHPP, but that was the limit of training and education envisaged. However, at the transition and sustainability stages, training was self-evidently required on how to effectively set up and run their MHPP Organisation: training in finance, business development, contract negotiation and so on. This training is itself empowering, but more than that, it brings communities into contact with a broader network of expertise and connection, which could, for example, link them to tourist organisations. At the sustainability stage, ongoing training and education is needed if the potential of their MPP is to be fully realised.

Universities and colleges are part of the wider education and training network. This opens opportunities for student involvement – the first micro-hydro project in Kedungrong Hamlet was built by student volunteers. It also opens up opportunities for research, as this project shows, and for fuller collaborations in solving some of the real problems that rural communities face as they develop and to capitalise on the knowledge they can contribute. For example, traditional farming practices are now recognised as crucial in preserving sustainable agriculture, particularly in the light of climate change.

Our last learning is that there is so much more to learn. It has been a privilege to share over a two-year period, the working, home and community lives of the hamlets of Kalisonggo, Blumbang and Kedungrong and their frustrations and aspirations. Likewise, we are grateful for the opportunity to gain insights into the enormous challenges that Governments face when they wish to better the lives of their citizens. The experience has been both humbling and uplifting and we relish the opportunity to do more.

And finally...

Our hope that this book will help working practitioners in development and communication. Yours is an enormous and important job and we trust that the practical tools we have developed here will be helpful to you. To those students who are studying these fields, our hope is you will begin to understand the complexities involved in development work and participatory communication. Should you choose to seek a career in this area, we can think of very few that will be more satisfying. You will help to change peoples' lives and if you do your job well, it will be for the better.

Note

1 Maslow's hierarchy of needs, although challenged by some, still remains a key reference for understanding motivation. His basic contention is that having fulfilled basic needs such as for food, water, shelter and security, people aspire to satisfy higher level needs such as a sense of belonging to social groups, a desire for respect and recognition and at the highest level concern for personal growth and the fulfilment of potential. His key writings are Maslow, A. H. (1943). A theory of human motivation. *Psychological Review,* 50 (4), 370–396; Maslow, A. H. (1954). *Motivation and personality.* Harper and Row: New York.

Index

Note: *Italicized* and **bold** pages refer to figures and tables respectively, and page numbers followed by "n" refer to notes.

Printed in the United States
by Baker & Taylor Publisher Services